Don't Muzzle The Ox!

All the Things a Pastor Wishes His
Church Understood but Is Hesitant
to Tell Them

Don't Muzzle The Ox!

All the Things a Pastor Wishes His Church Understood but Is Hesitant to Tell Them

Word of His Mouth Publishers
Mooresboro, NC

All Scripture quotations are taken from the **King James Version** of the Bible.

Some names have been changed to protect the identity of these individuals.

ISBN: 978-0-615-51899-2
Printed in the United States of America
© 2011 Dr. Bo Wagner (Robert Arthur Wagner)

Word of His Mouth Publishers
Mooresboro, NC
www.wordofhismouth.com

Recommendations

"Every once in a while, a book comes along that is both theological and practical. I encourage every pastor to buy this book to give it to his members. What an eye opener! Thank you, Bro. Bo, for this insightful book."

~Dr. Ronnie Simpson, Ph.D.~
Pastor Bright Light Baptist Church, Concord, NC
President Macedonia Baptist College

"I have been blessed with a great Pastor and a great church that takes care of my every need and respects my personal and private time as well. However, there are men who need help; they just don't know how to communicate that need. In this book, Dr. Wagner covers topics that most pastors are afraid to deal with. This book is a one-of-a-kind that could help any church to understand the needs of their pastor, the role his family plays, and the role that the church member is to play in helping the Man of God do what he is called to do, PASTOR THE CHURCH!"

~Assistant Pastor Michael Lindsay~
Love Valley Baptist Church, Kings Mountain, NC

"It takes a thoughtful man concerned for the ministries of others to write what he believes every church should know and practice. I found this book to be what I would desire all of our people know and understand."

~Pastor Jim Neeson~
Boomer Baptist Church, Boomer WV

"Dr. Wagner has treated this vital subject through Biblical application and personal illustrations. This volume is a must read for deacons and laymen alike. It is indeed necessary that local churches recognize the neglect of these vital truths and return to them immediately!"

~Dr. Tommy Wensil~
Unity Baptist Church, Kannapolis, NC

"Thank you for taking the time and effort to write on such a needy and timely subject. I thoroughly enjoyed reading your book and felt that there was a tremendous balance of honesty and humor in dealing with such an avoided and controversial subject. Every church member should read and take to heart the material in this book. If they did so I have no doubt our preachers and churches would be much more unified, strengthened and blessed. Thank you for your time, energy, and sacrifice for other men of God in writing and publishing this book."

~Pastor Bryan Treadway~
Emmanuel Baptist Church, Abingdon, VA

Don't Muzzle the Ox is a must read for every deacon and church member that desires to be a help instead of a hindrance to their pastor. Lord, raise up more Christians to hold up the hands of the man of God."

~Evangelist Davy Shelton~
Asheville, NC

"It is a joy to recommend to you Dr. Bo Wagner's book *DON'T MUZZLE THE OX*. Written by an experienced pastor teaching timely truths concerning the proper respect and treatment of the man of God. The book is a must read for every Christian who is interested in being a well pleasing servant to the Lord."

~Pastor Anthony Dye~
Mt. Zion Baptist Church, Hiawassee, GA

"Countless books have been written to guide the church into deeper spiritual growth. I have read many of those books and have found them very helpful in one way or another. Then, why another one? Because there are some issues that seem too sensitive for preachers to address in their own pulpits without coming across as selfish or self-centered though these topics are Biblical. Well, this book dares to tread into those areas that have been avoided way too long by our churches. Dr. Bo Wagner draws from a wealth of learning that has been filtered through the grid of personal experience to share many insights with us. The goal is not just to address these concerns that are often overlooked, as important as that is, but the spiritual development of both the pastor and congregation. Don't speed-read this book. Pause, ponder, pray, and grow!"

~Pastor Marc Williamson~
Carolina Baptist Church, Spartanburg, SC

"I just finished *Don't Muzzle the Ox*. Excellent work, Spirit-filled, this needs to be in the hands of God's people everywhere. Keep up the good work."

~Pastor Gary Gibson~
Open Door Baptist Church, Lexington, NC

"The reception of the seed sown by the sower will be determined by the condition of the soil. That parabolic truth verifies that how the reader responds to the scriptural truths which Dr. Wagner presents in this excellent book will speak volumes about the true spiritual condition of their heart. May the seed germinate and bear much fruit among Bible believing churches."

~Pastor Gene Rowell ~
Gants Street Baptist Church, Caysee, SC

This book has really helped several of my men, who now back me in every way better than they ever have. My youth pastor took it, on his own, and has been teaching it to our teen boys, so that he can help raise up a next generation of men to hold up the arms of the Man of God.

~Pastor Tom Fields~
Bethany Baptist Church, Thomasville, NC

This book changed my view of the Man of God. It helped me realize how much precious time he devotes to studying, visiting, soul winning, praying for me, my family, others in the church and lost souls. The Man of God and his wife and family needs our love and support in their times of need as much as I need his. It has helped me learn that God will bless a church that takes care of the Man of God and his family.

~Kevin Brewer~
Layperson, Thomasville, NC

Table of Content

Dedication

I alone, among all the pastors of Earth, have discovered a way to have a church of 1000 members without any of those members every causing me an ounce of grief. I am going to clone Christine Owens 999 times. This book is affectionately dedicated to our dear church grandmother, Christine Owens. She has been with us since the first day of our church. She has stayed when others close to her have left. She has defended us when others have attacked us. She has loved us, prayed for us, spoken up for us, and cheered us on at every turn. She remembers everything good we have ever done and chooses to forget any mistakes that we have ever made. Mrs. Christine, my wife and I love you dearly, and we are praying that you live to be 110!

Author's Note

Every state will have different laws concerning Pastoral compensation, and those laws often change. As you strive to follow any financial suggestions given in this book, please check with a good accountant to make sure you do so within the guidelines allowed by law.

Introduction

I have been a pastor for a great many years now. I count each of those years a blessing, though some years have been easier than others! Through all of those years, though, I have come to learn some things. There is a certain subject that pastors are very hesitant to cover, because it seems to be self-serving to them. They do not mind preaching on sin or salvation or sanctification or Heaven or even Hell. But when it comes to the subject of how the church is supposed to relate to the pastor and his family (which is, in fact, a Biblical subject!) suddenly the man of God begins to hesitate. How can he preach on the salary of the pastor or the respect that he and his family are due or a multitude of other like topics? This is certainly a conundrum.

And that is the reason for this book.

God has recently impressed upon my heart the need for this book to be written. I have a very good church; I love my church family! Through the years, they have done a wonderful job of taking care of us and relating well to us. I am very blessed to be their pastor. But that is not the case everywhere. There are good men of God across the land whose churches simply do not know what they are supposed to be doing or not doing in regards to their pastor and his family. And those good men of God usually leave the subject untouched from the pulpit out of fear of being seen as self-serving. But the topic is Biblical, and God always blesses a church that does right by His man.

So, with high hopes that churches and pastors everywhere will benefit from this book, I commend this work to the Lord and trust that He will breathe life into it!

Chapter One

Pastor and Wife Do Not Come as a "Two Employees for the Price of One" Package Deal

Everyone loves a bargain. This truth manifests itself differently from person to person and group to group. I myself am an avid yard-saler. What could be better than getting up early on a Saturday morning and burning up a tank of gas running all over town buying things that you don't exactly need but figure you may eventually find a use for? Who doesn't need a used "Ab Roller?" Why, for just five dollars, you can have that fine piece of equipment that the portly guy in the Dale, Jr. shirt paid $49.95 for less than a year ago! It should fit nicely right beside the treadmill you are using as a place to hang up your yard sale bought Polo shirts! What a bargain!

Bargains like that may not be very sensible, but at least they are not overtly unbiblical either. But in the local church, there is often a much more troublesome sort of bargain hunting. It is the sort of bargain hunting that well-meaning churches often engage in when seeking a pastor. The thought process goes something like this:

If we hire Reverend Feeblmeister, his wife Dorothy can be the church cleaning lady for us at no extra charge!

If we hire Reverend Thimblethorpe, his wife Martha can be the church secretary for us at no extra charge!

If we hire the Reverend Dwiblewood, his wife Louise can work in the church day care at no extra charge!

This is among the most demeaning things a church ever does to a pastor and his dear wife. It is demeaning to her by assuming that her time and efforts are worth nothing. It is demeaning to him by inferring that without his wife as a freebie employee, he himself would not be worth hiring. Look carefully at what the Scripture says:

KJV 1 Corinthians 9:1 *Am I not an apostle? am I not free? have I not seen Jesus Christ our Lord? are not ye my work in the Lord?* **2** *If I be not an apostle unto others, yet doubtless I am to you: for the seal of mine apostleship are ye in the Lord.* **3** *Mine answer to them that do examine me is this,* **4** *Have we not power to eat and to drink?* **5** *Have we not power to lead about* *a sister, a wife, as well as other apostles, and as the brethren of the Lord, and Cephas?* **6** *Or I only and Barnabas, have not we power to forbear working?* **7** *Who goeth a warfare any time at his own charges? who planteth a vineyard, and eateth not of the fruit thereof? or who feedeth a flock, and eateth not of the milk of the flock?* **8** *Say I these things as a man? or saith not the law the same also?* **9** *For it is written in the law of Moses, Thou shalt not muzzle the mouth of the ox that treadeth out the corn. Doth God take care for oxen?* **10** *Or saith he it altogether for our sakes? For our sakes, no doubt, this is written: that he that ploweth should plow in hope; and that he that thresheth in hope should be partaker of his hope.* **11** *If we have sown unto you spiritual things, is it a great thing if we shall reap your carnal things?*

The subject at hand was that of whether or not people should be paid for working in the ministry. Paul answered the question quite clearly by citing the Law of Moses. An ox should never be muzzled when he is treading out the corn; he should be allowed to benefit from the work he is doing. That was not written for the sake of oxen; it was written for the sake of those who serve in any capacity in the ministry as an employee, be it a pastor, a secretary, or a groundskeeper.

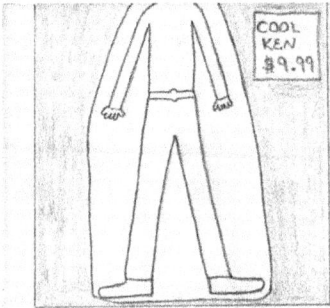

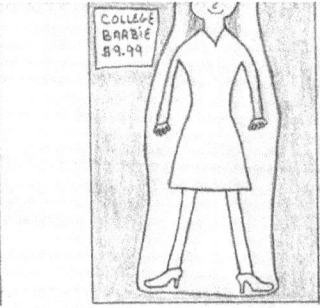

Years ago my wife was working a very high paying job. She had graduated from college with a secretarial degree, and shortly after we married, was hired on by a cellular company. I ran my own business, and she was bringing home more than I did! But then in 1997 I started the Cornerstone Baptist Church of Mooresboro, NC.

Within just a few months, the church was growing well, and I was beginning to be overrun with paperwork, which was not my strong suit anyway! My dear wife got under a burden for this wonderful problem in this fledgling work, and she came to me one day with a suggestion. What would I think, she inquired, about her quitting her high paying job and becoming the full time church secretary? After about three and a half seconds of intense praying I said, "Oh pleasepleasepleasepleaseplease do!" You see, I had already figured out that I was not up to the task of being both the pastor and the secretary, and I knew the incredible skill-set that she possessed. She is a numbers genius, a computer guru, and extremely organized. All of these skills that had secured her such a high-paying secular job would be an incredible asset to this budding church!

So, stepping out on faith, Dana and I approached the church, and suggested that she become the church secretary. We knew that there was no way they could pay her as yet; they were not even able to pay me. In fact, money from my business largely funded the church in those early years.

The church loved the idea, and I adored it. One of the reasons I liked it so well is, I must confess, a fleshly one. I figured that if I was going to be tempted to chase a secretary around the desk, I may as well be allowed to catch her! Having her as the church secretary has proven to be one of the wisest decisions my church and I ever made. It has guarded my testimony flawlessly, and she has done exactly the incredible job I knew she would. I realize that not every church and pastor takes this approach, but it has surely worked well for us.

For the first few years, my wife worked for free. But then one day, as the church grew, they began to look at the volume of work she was doing, and it dawned on them that they should be paying her. Now, we are still a relatively modest sized church, a bit under 200 as of the writing of this book. Through the years, the church has increased my salary to the point where I am full time, and they have increased Dana's salary some as well. Truthfully though, she is still a bargain. My wife is paid $300.00 a week to be the full time church secretary, a job at which she works on average around 60 hours a week. Day after day she works, and then night after night she brings the computer home and continues to work well into the night. Her duties as secretary are immense, mostly because she is good at absolutely everything! She does all of the church paper work, she edits and produces the weekly radio broadcast, she handles all correspondence with visitors, pastors, churches, missionaries, etc. She maintains the church web site, she cleans, she makes visits with me, she edits all of my lessons and books, she compiles my sermons into booklet form for me to use in the pulpit, she produces all of the giving statements, she uses databases to track attendance, and I could go on and on and on. She doesn't mind. She doesn't mind the long hours, and she doesn't mind the fact that she makes far less than she could in a secular job with her degree and her abilities. The church is paying her what they can, and she loves them!

But let me tell you what she does mind...

One day, a gentleman was discussing my salary as pastor. The gentleman is no longer with us, but we loved him while he was and love him still. On this particular day, though, he made a statement that caused a rather "strong reaction" from my dear wife. The statement he made was, "Well, you can't just count what we are giving the pastor, you have to count his wife's salary as something we are giving him too!"

Friend, let me tell you, when I told Dana that, she went ballistic! I mean she bounced from the floor to the wall, onto the bookshelf, onto the ceiling fan, made about half a dozen laps, and then rocketed back down to the ground. When she landed, she said, "And what exactly does he think? Am I chopped liver or something? Does he think my sixty hours a week of work should count for nothing? How dare he say such a thing!" I could not argue with a word of what she said, first of all because she was absolutely right, and secondly because I had already done the floor/wall/bookshelf/ceiling fan/floor circuit myself when he first said it!

Even the use of the word "give" in that regard is demeaning and inappropriate. A church does not "give" a pastor or secretary anything, anymore than a factory "gives" an employee a salary. In both cases there is a job that needs to be done, and the people fulfilling those jobs *earn* a paycheck.

People would do well to use a modicum of logic before they make such statements or assumptions. Most pastors' wives who do work for the church do so at a far less salary than they could make in a secular job setting. Most pastors' wives are exceptionally skilled in a great variety of fields. All of them are willing to work for free, *but none of them should ever have to if the church can afford to hire them!* And none of them should ever, ever have to be so insulted as to be told that their salary for their work is simply an act of generosity towards her husband! Think about it. What if the man who said those words, let's say he works at the Acme Widgett company, was approached by his boss, who had this to say to him:

> *Bob, you have been doing a good job and we would like to give you a raise. So what we are going to do is allow your wife to come work for us full time, and we will count her salary as a raise for you!*

How do you think "Bob" would respond to that? I think the answer is obvious! Both Bob and his wife would be highly insulted, and rightfully so. Bob is working hard to earn his own salary and his own raises.

If they want Bob's wife to come on board, that should not change one iota of what they should be doing for Bob all by himself!

What every church body should know, and what every pastor would like to be able to say to them, is that he, by himself, should be earning his own salary, and that if his wife chooses to work at the church, she should be paid well for it, and her salary should never be counted as part of his salary. Every pastor I know, as well as every pastor's wife, would be willing to work for free for the Lord in the church if they needed to. But none should have to if the church can afford to hire them! The pastor and his wife are not a "two employees for the price of one" package deal.

Chapter Two

"Full Time" Should Not Mean Radically Different Things for Pastors and Factory Workers

The words "I am full time" are magical in the ministry. I remember well when I was able to speak them for the first time. It was just a couple of years into the history of our church, and we were finally able to shut down our jewelry store and be supported by my salary from the church. Friend, a pastor feels like he has "arrived" at that point! He is on top of the world, and nothing can ever go wrong again...

Yes, you are correct, that feeling did not last long! To this day I still enjoy being full time in the ministry, but it did not take me very long to learn that members in the pew often view a full time pastor in an entirely different light than they view themselves as full time factory workers, plumbers, electricians, etc. For workers all over America, including those that sit on the pews of our churches, "full time" has a very specific meaning. A full time worker is a person who works forty hours a week and then has the rest of the hours a week as his own personal time in which he can do whatever he chooses. If that full time worker works more than forty hours a week, he is then regarded as "working overtime" and is paid a considerable amount more per hour, usually "time and a half."

But that is not what church members expect of their pastors. When a full time worker sitting on a pew looks at his full time pastor standing behind the pulpit, that member usually expects something radically different of his pastor than he does of himself. If it were actually verbalized, most members view the "full time" of their pastors this way:

My pastor is full time at the church, which means that every waking moment of his life should be dedicated to this church. My pastor is never allowed to do any other work on the side to earn extra money, because he is full time here. My pastor needs to stay off of the golf course, because he is full time here. My pastor needs to keep regular office hours Monday through Friday, visit all day on Saturday, work all day on Sunday, be on call 24/7, and make emergency hospital visits in the middle of the night, because he is our "full time pastor."

This really is the way that many church members view their pastors! But do you see the incredible double standard? They demand to work a simple forty hours and then have the other 128 hours of the week to do whatever in the world they want. If they want to do some extra work on the side to earn money that is fine, because they have already done their "full time job" for the week. If they want to take a couple of days and go camping or golfing that is fine, because they have already done their "full time job" for the week. If they want to join the Y or play a sport or have a hobby in their off hours that is fine because they have already done their "full time job" for the week. But that same right is then looked down on in regards to their pastor!

Now, any good pastor understands that he is, in fact, on call 24 hours a day, seven days a week. Any good pastor understands that he is going to have to work way more than 40 hours most weeks. My regular habit for the past fourteen years has been to average a 70-80 hour work week or more. That may sound unbelievable, but a simple look at the average work week will show it to be true.

On Sunday, my work day will start around 8 a.m. making final preparations for the morning service. I will then teach Sunday school and preach the morning service. I will be the last one to leave after the service is over. My family and I will go grab a quick bite of lunch and then I will sit down at my laptop the rest of the afternoon making final preparations for the evening service. I will come back to church to make sure it is clean, lead the early youth program, lead the choir practice after that, and then we will have service. After service, I will once again be the last one to leave, usually after talking to several individuals who need my time and advice. I will go home, eat a quick bite, open the laptop again, and do wrap up work for the day, recording pertinent details about all that happened. I will usually close the computer down around 11 p.m. Even deducting two hours during the day for eating, which is not usually anywhere near that much time, I have still worked 13 hours by the time the first day of the week is done.

On Monday through Friday I will get to the office around 9 a.m. and will either work at my desk preparing messages or work on things that need fixing around the church and will usually wrap that up around six. We will also run whatever church errands need to be run and make whatever known visits we need to make. Deducting an hour for lunch, which is another 40 hours of work, bringing the total to 53 so far. On Mondays after six I usually do counseling, which adds another two hours or so, for a total of 55. On Wednesday I will be at church till 9 p.m. or so, adding another three hours, for a total of 58. On Thursdays I will do a gym outreach that we have been running for ten years now, adding another three hours, bringing the total to 61 hours. On Saturday I will do visitation at 9:30 a.m. then usually go back to the church and work till 3 p.m. or so, adding another six hours, for a total of 67 hours. At night, sitting in front of my computer, I will usually add another two hours or so of work late into the night five nights of the week adding another ten hours or so for a total of 77. And usually, at least once a week, there will be a late night call necessitating me going to the hospital, rounding the week out at 80.

Now, please understand that some weeks are a bit less, maybe 50 or 60, others actually a bit more. During the two and a half years I was building our church building, I averaged more than ninety hours a week.

By the way, you may have noticed that I did not list any days off in my reckoning. Please, do not write me any nasty letters for what I am about to say, but even though I know that I should, I do not usually take any days off. (Put down the phone, Mom, I know it's wrong, I know I am going to have a nervous breakdown one day, and I promise I will do better. Someday.) Instead of taking a regular day off, I will work for a couple of months straight and then take two or three days and go out of town. And it is at that point that we have in the past encountered the problem of having our "full time" regarded radically different that anyone else's full time. We have been accused of "always being on vacation!" But you see, each week, we work the hours of two full time work weeks and only get paid for one! We do not mind a bit, I love the church, and I love to work. But when I want to take a couple of days off, or even a week, I have certainly built up enough time to do so.

Another way that this difference manifests itself is when a pastor preaches a revival meeting. I have actually known of people who believed that the pastor should give any love offering he gets to the church, since the church is already paying him a "full time" salary. But what would it be like if the same expectation were applied to them?

Bob, you are a full time employee here at the Acme Rubber Chicken Factory, are you not?

Why yes, Mr. Noodlesoup, I am.

Then why have you not given us the money that you made when you cut your neighbor's lawn last Saturday?

But Mr. Noodlesoup, I did that in my free time, I had already worked my forty hours here!

That's no excuse, Bob; you are a full time employee here, which means you are not allowed to earn any money doing anything else in your free time.

I suspect that rubber chicken maker Bob would have a real problem with that expectation. Pastor Bob does as well, though! Look at what the Bible says:

KJV Proverbs 11:1 *A false balance is abomination to the LORD: but a just weight is his delight.*

Simply put, God expects things to be handled evenly! He does not expect "full time" to mean radically different things concerning pastors and parishioners.

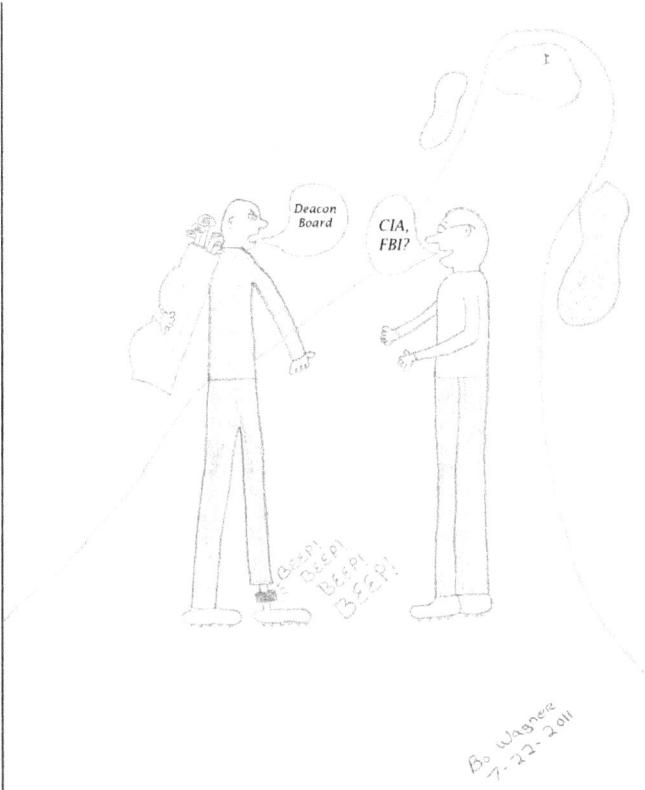

29

Now, please, understand every good pastor knows that most churches cannot afford to pay them by the hour. I have an earned doctorate, as do many pastors. If a church paid a pastor say, $20.00 an hour, which is certainly no lavish wage these days, he would make $800.00 a week for forty hours. But then from hour 40-80, he would earn time and a half, meaning he would make another $1200 for those hours. That would be a salary of $2000 a week if a church paid a well-trained pastor by the hour! The vast majority of churches cannot afford that or anywhere near it, so they place their pastor on salary instead, meaning that no matter how many hours he works, he only makes a set amount.

Most pastors are quite willing to live with this arrangement, since they are called by God to be in the ministry. If the average church added up what their pastor was making by the hour, though, they would probably be inclined to be a little nicer to him!

Being on salary for a pastor has one, and only one, perk. The money is certainly not a perk, since we have already established that most pastors work for minimum wage or less. The one perk a pastor has being on salary, full time at his church, is freedom of schedule. If he wants to preach a revival meeting and earn some extra money, he has the right to do so. If he wants to cut lawns and earn some extra money, he has the right to do so. If he wants to golf a couple of days a week, he has the right to do so. If he wants to spend a couple of hours a day at the gym, he has the right to do so.

And by the way, I would be negligent if I failed to mention that even when a pastor preaches a revival meeting, he still will end up working forty or more hours for his own church that week! A few weeks back from the time that I am writing this, I preached a revival in Fayetteville, NC, Monday through Friday. On the Sunday before I left, I put in my typical 13 hour day. On Monday, I worked 6 more hours at the church before I left, bringing the total to 19. On Tuesday, I drove back to Gastonia for a surgery of a church member, and then back again, adding another 8 hours, for a total of 27. Tuesday through Friday, I spent two hours a day preparing messages and lessons for the following Sunday, adding 8 hours, for a total of 35. On Saturday, I spent another 7 hours on the laptop preparing for the next day, bringing it to a total of 42 hours!

This is by no means uncommon. Pastors all across the land do the exact same thing. What people see from their pastor is three hours of work on Sunday. What they do not see is the numerous hours that preceded the Sunday! Whenever I meet someone who cracks wise about "the pastor earning good money to work three hours a week," I always pray that God will send that person into the ministry, so that I can crack wise on how quickly the know-it-all figures out how wrong he was!

Church member, please do not ever take for granted the many hours that your pastor works and just how little he does it for. If he wants to golf, let him. If he wants to preach revival meetings, let him. And if you cannot let him, then by all means, go into the ministry yourself so that he can smile at how quickly you learn just how wrong you have been!

Chapter Three

If You Believe It Is Your Job to Keep the Preacher Poor so that God Can Keep Him Humble, Then God Needs to Keep You Mute to Keep the Preacher Sane!

Relax; this book will deal with a great many things other than money. But since the salary of the pastor is one of the main things he hesitates to mention, I want to make sure that I say everything that needs to be said in this book. Let us begin this chapter with a verse of Scripture:

KJV 1 Timothy 5:17 *Let the elders that rule well be counted worthy of double honour, especially they who labour in the word and doctrine.* **18** *For the scripture saith, Thou shalt not muzzle the ox that treadeth out the corn. And, The labourer is worthy of his reward.*

The terms elder, bishop, and pastor in the Scripture are interchangeable, and all refer to one thing, the office of the pastor. In I Timothy 5:17-18, Paul gave commandment concerning the salary of the pastor, especially a pastor who really works at studying his Bible and preparing good messages. The commandment he gave was that such a pastor should be regarded as worthy of "double honor." The verse that follows shows us clearly that he was speaking of money–the reward of the laborer. The word honor itself tells us the exact same thing. It is from the word *timay,* and it means "a price paid." We get our English word "honorarium" from it. Quite simply, Paul was saying that a good pastor should be regarded as worthy of a double paycheck! He should be a highly paid individual in regards to what his church members make. He should be among the upper income earners in the church.

This runs contrary, unfortunately, to what a great many churches believe about their pastor. Somehow they have gotten the idea that the pastor is to be kept poor and that it is good for him. They believe, in fact, that it is their job to keep him as poor as possible. My father-in-law preached a meeting once upon a time at a church to which he had never been. He was met in the parking lot by the deacons, who immediately began to brag to him that the church had over a million dollars in the bank. Shortly thereafter, my father-in-law met the pastor of the church. He drove up in an old, run-down vehicle with bald tires. Some further "snooping" revealed that this poor pastor was being given a fast-food worker level salary by this church.

Now, being somewhat less than patient with such garbage, my father-in-law absolutely let those deacons have it. I mean he blistered their sorry hides, and rightfully so! Any church that has the means to do so ought to treat their pastor well; he should be regarded as worthy of double honor. And even a church that does not have the means to do so will be pleased to discover, if they have enough faith to try it out, that God will bless a church that steps out on faith and treats their pastor well. My own church discovered this in the early years, often giving me raises when the money was not there to do so. Time and again, God increased the offerings to cover those raises.

The membership of churches generally falls into one category or the other. Either they greedily hold onto each penny they can, trying to spend as little on a pastor as possible, or they joyously and generously treat their pastor as well financially as possible, realizing that God will bless the church that blesses His man.

Once again, please consider how the average member in the pew would feel if they were treated at work the way they treat their pastor:

> *Bob, we appreciate your work here at the Acme Fungal Funnel Company. Without you, a great many fungi would still be running rampant in our land, unable to be funneled into a proper containment unit. And so, Bob, in appreciation of all of your hard*

In light of your years of service, the board has voted to give you a little something extra. . .

work, we are going to let you work 70-80 hours a week, and we are going to expect you to be on call 24/7, and we are going to pay you minimum wage. Isn't that great?

I am guessing that Bob would not regard that as great after all. He would rightly expect, doing a job so vital, to be treated very well. But, ladies and gentlemen, may I ask what job is more vital than that of a pastor? It is his preaching that will teach your children of their need for a Savior and keep them out of Hell. It is his counseling that will solidify and maybe even save your marriage. It is his comfort in times of bereavement that will keep you from giving up. Others look out for your body or for your creature comforts, but the man of God looks out for your soul!

If your pastor is on the high end of the earning curve in your church, let me commend you. You are doing right, please keep it up! But if your pastor is on the low end of the earning curve, let me challenge you. You can do better, much better, and God will bless you as you do.

Chapter Four

Considering the Roof over the Pastor's Head

Surprisingly enough, pastors are actually just like their members in one regard...they live in houses. Wait, wait, I know that you find that amazing and are right now writing me letters to tell me how incredibly astute I am. Put down those pens and keep reading because I have much more to say.

It is time that we consider the roof over the pastor's head, for there is much that needs to be said concerning it. The housing of the pastor falls into several basic categories.

One: The pastor lives in a parsonage on church property; the house and grounds are owned by the church.

Two: The pastor owns his own home on his own property or rents his own dwelling.

CHURCH

CHURCH MEMBER'S HOUSE

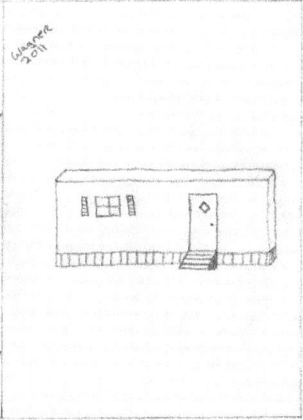

FELLOWSHIP HALL

PARSONAGE

40

Three: The church at some point buys or builds a house for their pastor.

Each of these categories have merits and each have drawbacks. Each will undergo consideration in this chapter and be given certain guidelines, things that the pastor often is hesitant to explain to his people.

Let us begin by examining the concept of the pastor living in a parsonage on church property. The benefits of such an arrangement are that the pastor does not have to use his salary for housing and that he is right there at the church where he can look after things. As far as I know, those are the only benefits.

The drawbacks of such an arrangement are more numerous. First, it leaves the pastor in a situation where at any moment, even after 20 or 30 years of ministry, he and his family could instantly become homeless. When a pastor resigns or is asked to leave, the parsonage does not go with him. If the pastor dies, even after decades of ministry, the new pastor will expect to live in the parsonage, leaving the dear pastor's wife homeless, and likely with no way to earn an income of her own. These drawbacks alone truly make this the least desirable of all of the housing options of a pastor. What member would want to live in those same conditions?

But another drawback, far more subtle than the first, is that the membership will inevitably refuse to regard the parsonage as "the pastor's house," regarding it instead as "church property." What this means in practical terms is that they will normally refuse to give the pastor and his family the same privacy and liberty that they themselves expect in their own homes.

My wife was a PK (pastor's kid) and later became an MK (missionary's kid). While she was a PK, her family lived in a parsonage. As regular as clockwork, bright and early every Saturday morning, a man in the church would knock on their door (opening it as he knocked!) and ask to come in and have breakfast with them! My in-laws would let the man come in. As a little girl my wife would have to run to her room and get out of her PJs and put on her regular clothes, not being able to relax on Saturday mornings like the other kids in church. They could also not cook out on the grill without grilling lots of extra food, because as soon as people saw them in the yard they would stop and expect to eat with them. Horror stories like that can be told by almost every parsonage-dwelling person in America.

And what of painting or decorating? The answer is almost always the same. The regular person in the pew just does whatever they want. The parsonage-dwelling pastor must go before some church committee and get permission before they paint, renovate, or even decorate. After all, it is "church property!"

No member would ever want to live like that, and if there is another option, no pastor ever should have to live like that. If something other than a parsonage can be arranged, please do so!

Option number two was having the pastor own or rent his own home. Once again there are drawbacks and benefits to this arrangement. In this one, though, there are far fewer drawbacks than in the first.

The main drawback to this arrangement is that it is another expense for the pastor. The good news is, if the church pays the pastor well, this should not be a problem. The benefits to such an arrangement, though, are numerous. In short, none of the problems that exist in a parsonage situation exist in this one. The pastor can retire or be asked to leave, and he still has his own home. He can die, and his wife still has a home. He has his privacy and the right to do what he pleases to the home, because it is his.

Option number three was for the church to eventually buy or build their pastor a house. The church I was sent out of to start Cornerstone really did well in regards to this. For his ten year anniversary as pastor, they built the pastor and his wife a home in the mountains and gave it to them. Then about ten years later, they built a new parsonage beside the church for him to live in during the week! Talk about the best of both worlds!

If a church is able, and a good many are, they should eventually build or buy the pastor a house. The pastor will spend most of his life building the church, physically, spiritually, and most every other way. He will often neglect his own house in favor of tending to the house of God. Any church that can bless their good pastor by building or buying him a house is investing in a worthwhile cause! Think about it: a pastor who has been given a home in which to live is not likely to ever be lured away by another church! This option has no drawbacks that I know of, provided the church is able to afford it, and yet has every benefit imaginable.

No matter which option a church and pastor chooses, the pastor deserves the same privacy in his home that every member deserves in theirs. If you are a member of a church whose pastor lives in a parsonage on church property, take it upon yourself to make sure that the pastor and his family are given as much privacy in that home as if they lived in the wilderness. It is what you want where you live, and it is what he wants where he lives!

This concept of the man of God being provided with housing by his congregation is not a new one. It has been around for many thousands of years and can be seen in the Bible as far back as the time of the Exodus. Look at what God commanded concerning the Levites:

KJV Numbers 35:1 *And the LORD spake unto Moses in the plains of Moab by Jordan near Jericho, saying,* **2** *Command the children of Israel, that they give unto the Levites of the inheritance of their possession cities to dwell in; and ye shall give also unto the Levites suburbs for the cities round about them.* **3** *And the cities shall they have to dwell in; and the suburbs of them shall be for their cattle, and for their goods, and for all their beasts.*

The Levites, the men of God, were given entire cities and suburbs to live in, by commandment of God. They gave their lives in ministry for the people, and the people responded by making sure they had roofs over their head. A church today does well to follow that pattern, making sure that a pastor has a home that is large enough for his family, has plenty of privacy, and can never be taken away from him.

Chapter Five

Round, Round, Round, Round Your Pastor Gets Around, and You Need to Help Him Get There!

Ah, the luxury of working at the Acme Acne Alleviation Medication Plant:

Honey, what are you doing there at the table with that paper and pencil?

Oh, I'm just working on a part of our budget.

What part are you working on?

Gasoline for the vehicles.

Well that should be easy.

Yep, that's why I started here. 5 miles to work each day, 5 miles back, that equals 10 miles a day, 5 days a week, 50 miles. Add in 30 or so miles on the weekend to go back and forth to church and whatever running around we need to do, and we are looking at 80 miles a week. The car gets 20 miles to the gallon, so we are looking at four gallons a week, at 4 dollars a gallon, 16 dollars a week. That was easy!

I know and you know that most people will drive a bit more than 80 miles a week. My point is that whatever miles the regular church member/factory worker drives, they are usually very predictable miles. The average church member/factory worker knows how much they will need for gas each week, and how many miles they will put on their car each week, and therefore, how long that vehicle will likely last.

Not so the pastor.

Pastors are put into a unique conundrum. They are on a fixed income. Remember, as I pointed out earlier, unlike the average church member/factory worker, the pastor does not make any more for working overtime. So they have a fixed income with which to work, but they also have entirely unpredictable miles that they are expected to drive...usually a huge amount of miles! The pastor does not simply drive to and from church. He drives back and forth into town gathering supplies, he drives mile after mile visiting church members, he drives mile after mile knocking on doors telling people about Jesus, and he drives mile after mile visiting a dozen different hospitals. Every time someone has surgery or a kidney stone or an accident or a baby or a hundred other things, the pastor will be summoned to get into his vehicle and show up. No member in the pew has that problem/responsibility. I regularly put more than 50,000 miles per year on my vehicle, and the church (rightfully) expects it! If I did not come to a surgery because I did not have enough gas to get there, my members would be most unhappy.

And in this, may I give a huge pat on the back to my dear Cornerstone family! Way back in 1999, early in the history of the church, some very godly, far-sighted men decided to ensure that would never be a problem. They voted to have the church provide all of the gas for my wife and myself. Way to go Cornerstone! In so doing, I have never, EVER had to miss a hospital visit for want of gas money in the budget. And buddy, have there been a lot of very long distance hospital visits! My church is in the thriving metropolis of Mooresboro, NC, population 276. From that starting point, I have made hospital visits to Chapel Hill (3 hours away) Shelby (15 minutes away) Kings Mountain (30 minutes away) Gastonia (40 minutes away) Charlotte (1 hour away) Spartanburg (45 minutes away) Greenville (1 hour away) Rutherfordton (20 minutes away) Hendersonville (45 minutes away) Asheville (1 ½ hours away) and many, many more. I have also preached funerals as far away as Arlington National Cemetery, eight hours away!

But wait, friends, there's more...

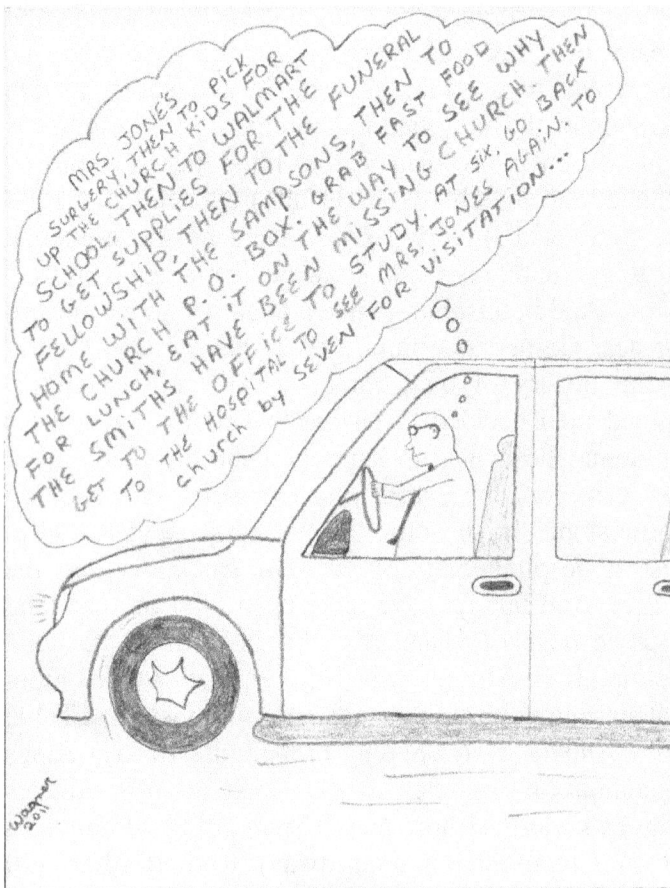

Typical pastor out "blowing" the church's gas money.

I have traveled to New Jersey, twice, to pick up equipment for the church. I have traveled to St. Louis to look at pews for the church. I have traveled to Chicago to pick up a lift for the church. I have traveled to Georgia multiple times for carpet for the church. I also use my Yukon every day of the school year to carry not just my own children but other church children, as well, to Christian school across the state line.

Locally is just as bad. During our building project I made 5-6 trips a day to Lowe's getting supplies and materials. It is for all of these things and more that my church rightfully determined to put all of the gas in my vehicles. Once again, I cannot stress enough just how proper and right they were to do so! Any church that expects their pastor to drive unlimited miles on their behalf needs to give him the means to do so. The gas a church puts into the tank for a pastor is a business expense that allows him to fulfill the massive expectations they place on him and his vehicle.

But there is another aspect of this to look at, one that once again, my church got right. The average church member/factory worker puts very few miles on a vehicle, and thus their vehicle will last for a very long time. But since the church places expectations on the pastor that runs the miles up on his vehicle very, very fast, it is entirely appropriate for the church to provide a vehicle for the pastor if they are able. Even if it is a good used vehicle, it is just the right thing to do! My church did a couple of years ago, buying us a nine-year-old Yukon big enough to carry my entire family. It may be used, but we love it; our church did well!

The church that I came from is much older and much bigger than ours. Every two years or so they buy the pastor and his wife brand new vehicles. Good for them! Once again, God has shown that He will bless a church that takes care of His man. That church is not hurting a bit; they are thriving.

And now, please, let me say just a word or two about the inevitable internet auction aficionado that will surely rear his head when it does come time to buy the pastor a vehicle. Church, whoever and wherever you are, please restrain that person, even if you need to use duct tape to do it! (I am teasing, of course) There is perhaps nothing more inappropriate than a church with plenty of room in the budget that, for some reason, determines to buy a $300, 30-year-old Rambler for their pastor. To quote my church teens, "Seriously?"

If you expect your pastor to drive an insane amount of miles, if you expect him to get "round, round, round, round," make sure he is able to do so in comfort, in a vehicle that will not leave him stranded on the side of the road, and without any fear of seeing the needle ever touch the big red E.

Chapter Six

Mess with My Kids and You Mess with a Mama and Daddy, Not a Pastor and Pastor's Wife

I dearly love looking at "church cartoons." One of my very favorite ones shows one nursery worker changing a baby's diaper while she talks to another nursery worker. She looks over at the other worker and says, "Well, I would never have expected the pastor's child to have a diaper like this!" One of the things that make that so funny is that it is not too far off from the truth!

Pastor's children are usually in a terrible predicament. Their DNA has not altered one bit just because their parents are in the ministry. They are, to the core, regular children just like every other child. But unlike other children, they have two strikes against them from the moment they step up to the plate. First, they live in glass houses; their every movement is seen and scrutinized. Second, the expectations that people place on them are unrealistic. Church members usually expect angelic behavior out of flesh and blood children, simply because they are the offspring of the pastor.

When we started Cornerstone Baptist Church, there were no children. Within a few weeks we had a few kids coming, and that quickly grew into a sizeable youth group. For a few years, new kids came, but no babies were born. And then one day a lady in the church got pregnant. That lady was my wife! The first baby born into our church was my son. Still, a baby is not exactly part of the youth group. So for quite a few years, I was the pastor and youth pastor to a bunch of children that were not my own. I helped to raise them, I loved on them, I prayed for them, I rewarded them when they did right, and I scolded them when they did wrong. But in the back of my mind, I always knew that we had a potential problem brewing...

After my son, came two more daughters. These three kids absolutely light up my world; I love being their daddy! And finally, there came a day when they were old enough to be recognized as being part of the youth group. And when they did, I went before my church and gave them a little speech that I had been rehearsing in my mind for a great many years. It went something like this:

Dear church: I love you, and I am grateful to you for a great many things. One of the things I am grateful for is that you have allowed me to be a youth pastor to your children. I have loved them; I have been fair with them; I have sacrificed for them. Now I have a favor to ask of you. My own children are now becoming a part of the youth group that your children have grown up in. I want you to know something. The pastor's kids, who are now becoming a part of the youth group, have a mama and a daddy, just like your kids. My wife and I are that mama and daddy. We love our kids just like you love yours, and we will get defensive over our kids just like you have over yours if they are wronged. I want you to help me by letting my kids be average, regular, normal members of the youth group. I want you to help me by not expecting more of them than you did of your own kids. I want you to help me by not getting angry and crying "favoritism!" if they happen to win a trophy or earn a reward like yours have. I want you to help me by letting me or my wife be the one to yank them up if they need to be yanked up. I want you to help me by not watching them like hawks to try and catch them doing something wrong. I want you to help me by not expecting me to be harsher on them when they do wrong than I have been on your children. In short, please, do me the favor of letting my kids have a normal childhood here in our church.

The speech was magnificent, don't you think? I only wish the results had been as magnificent. Now, in most of my folks, they were. The vast majority of my members heeded what I asked and have abided by it very well. The vast majority of my people have allowed my wife and I to be the parents of our kids. The vast majority of my people have not placed unrealistic expectations on them just because they are pastor's kids. But, in saying the words "the vast

*And my little Johnny here just saw the Pastor's son
running in the church!*

majority," you have already figure out that there was a tiny minority that ignored most, if not all, of what I asked.

I remember a time a few years ago when I walked into the office, and my wife was as white as a sheet, shaking in rage, with a homicidal look on her face. Trust me, after a few years of marriage, a husband does, in fact, know what his wife's face looks like when she is seriously contemplating killing someone! I finally got her calmed down and found out what she was so livid over. It turns out that about fifteen minutes earlier, while I was detained in some other part of the church, she had walked into the big vestibule and run right up on a man in our church who was dragging my son by the forearm. Caleb had (as far as he was concerned) done something wrong, and this young man of about 27 or so had snatched him up in a tight grip and was dragging him somewhere to "deal with him." My wife immediately removed the man's hand from my son's arm and marched straight back to the office in order to avoid the temptation to claw the man's eyes out on the spot, which she figured would cause me trouble.

The man was gone by the time I became aware of what happened, and that is a good thing. When I saw the bruises on my son's little forearm, I came unglued and rushed out to find the man. I am not exaggerating when I tell you that, if he had still been there, I would have put that "dear man" in the hospital to give him time to consider the error of his ways! By the time he came back that night, I had cooled off enough (barely) to be able to speak to him sternly and tell him never to do that again.

Now consider this: do you think that man would have done that to any other child in church? The answer is no! Why did he feel free to do it to mine? Because he has in his mind that the pastor's kids are somehow "church property" and that anyone has the right and responsibility to discipline them. Sir, ma'am, church member of whatever church you attend, pay attention: the pastor's children have a daddy and a mama! And that daddy and mama are first and foremost parents to their children, and after that they are pastor and pastor's wife of a church. You need to treat the pastor's children with the same hands-off approach that you take with the deacon's kids or the choir director's kids or the factory worker who just shows up and sits on a pew's kids. Furthermore, you need to be willing to let them be actual children, not miniature adults. The fact that a pastor's children are children of a pastor does not mean that they will never burp out loud or run through the church or pass a note. They will. And the pastor, like any good father, will use those things as a way to teach his children right from wrong, proper from improper. But if you as a member become "righteously indignant" over such things, when you never became "righteously indignant" over your own children doing such things, then you are guilty of a double standard!

A few years ago we had a family ask to speak to me in my office. He and his wife sat down across from my desk, and he told me they were leaving the church. Naturally, I asked why. He replied, "Because you don't have your children under control." Now, please understand that my oldest child at the time was about 7! What, I wondered, could a seven year old have done bad enough to make this man leave the church? He replied, "A week ago, I had to come to you and tell you that he was running through the church."

I said, "Yes, you did, and I promptly spanked him for it, since I myself have told him not to do that."

He said, "That doesn't change the fact that he did, in fact, run through the church!"

At this point, I was actually wondering if I was hearing and understanding the man correctly. I said, "Sir, you told me that, and I told you that I dealt with him over that, and as far as I know, he hasn't done that anymore. If he does, I will spank him again. What exactly do you want from me as a parent other than to actually deal with my children when they do wrong?"

He said, "The pastor's kids should never do things like that, and since they do, we are leaving."

By this point, I was fit to be tied. So, knowing that they were leaving anyway, I availed myself of the opportunity to take a swing or two of my own. I said, "Sir, with all due respect, it is probably good that you do. My kids mean more to me than you do, and if I have to choose between them being here and you being here, I'll choose them. Secondly, sir, you might want to look to your own children. Your boy (he was about five) tried to kiss my little girl last week. I overlooked it, because I am willing to be patient with little kids that need to learn right from wrong. But since you don't seem to want to extend that same courtesy to me, let me just warn you that if he tries it again, I will call the police on him and file sexual harassment charges."

If I were the world's greatest artist, I would, at this point in this book, draw you a picture of the man's face when I said that. Just trust me when I tell you, I went to bed giggling that night, and I have never yet forgotten the shell-shocked look on his face.

One of the best things that a church can ever do for a pastor is to regard his children as precious souls to pray for and love rather than as targets to shoot at. Pastor's children have a much harder life than any other kids that you likely know. Lift them up, pray for them daily, cut them some slack, be patient with them when they fail, and cheer for them when they do something good. If you love your pastor's children, your pastor will love you! But if you choose to make targets out of them, you will find out the hard way that a mama and a daddy are a mama and a daddy, period, even if they happen to be the pastor and his wife.

Chapter Seven

Please Do Not Celebrate "Stupid People Day" While I Am on Vacation

I owe a debt of gratitude to a friend of mine, Pastor Wesley Webb. He is the man who told me about a little known and completely unscheduled national holiday, "Stupid People Day." On Stupid People Day, people who are normally rational and intelligent will act in completely ridiculous, irrational, illogical, or unbiblical ways. Absolutely everyone celebrates Stupid People Day at some point in their life. This does not mean they are stupid. The very definition that I gave above is that Stupid People Day is something that "rational" and "intelligent" people sometimes celebrate. In other words, people with perfectly good brains have a momentary lapse in judgment! Unfortunately for a great many pastors, Stupid People Day usually ends up occurring while we are on vacation!

A pastor has an incredibly stressful life. If the average church member only knew how many times a pastor will call another pastor and ask, "Why are we doing this?" it would probably shock them. Pastors have to hear husbands and wives fight and accuse each other, find a way to fix it for them, and then never tell anyone about the counseling session. Pastors have to get up in the middle of the night and rush to the hospital to "comfort" the sodden drunk who tried to kill himself by taking a bottle of multivitamins and is now having his stomach pumped. Pastors have to produce and deliver several good messages and lessons each week, and if they deliver a dud, they will hear about it. Pastors have to deal with the person on the left of the church threatening to leave because it is too cold in the auditorium, while the person on the right side of the church is complaining that it is too hot, and when he suggests that they switch sides, he gets accused of being flippant. Pastors have to visit the sick while trying to stay healthy themselves. Pastors have to go to sleep night after night with knots in their stomach over whoever happens to be mad at them for whatever reason this particular week. I could go on and on forever, but just please believe me when I tell you, a pastor really needs and really looks forward to vacation!

But alas, vacation for a church member and a church pastor usually do not end up with the same degree of peace and relaxation. Think about it, church member. When is the last time you were on vacation and got a call telling you that you needed to come back

Pastor Smith is on vacation this week! You go tell Mrs. Jones that Mrs. Wilson said she has bad breath, and I'll go tell Mrs. Wilson that Mrs. Jones said her kids are brats!

and preach a funeral? When is the last time you were on vacation and had to turn right around and come back for someone's emergency surgery?

But those things, friend, are not really that big of a deal to a pastor. The really big deal is when a pastor on vacation has to deal with people that have decided to observe "Stupid People Day" while he is away.

Many years ago, I was on a much needed vacation. On a church day, I did what I always do. My family and I went to church where we were, and after it was over, I called back to one of my members, and asked how church had gone back home. The hesitation in his voice let me know that I was not going to like what I was going to hear.

It seems that while I was gone, an adult with a teenage child had blown up at another adult with a teenage child over a trivial issue between the children. The kids were quickly fine, but the adults just came completely unglued! They took a small issue, made a nuclear episode over it, screamed and shouted like banshees for everybody to hear, and many others were quickly drawn into the fray. The entire service was ruined, and we were at risk of losing multiple families. It is after telling me all of this that the man said, "Preacher, be sure and don't worry about this; just enjoy the rest of your vacation."

Bwahahahahahahahahahahahahahahahahahahah ahahahahahahahahahahahahahaha! Have you ever heard a funnier joke? "Don't worry about this; just

64

enjoy the rest of your vacation?" Friends, I could have been on the Riviera with a million dollars to spend with my wife rubbing my back while Barry White crooned to us on the radio and a huge juicy steak was cooking on the grill beside me, and I would not have enjoyed any of it a bit! My vacation was thoroughly, completely, absolutely ruined; I thought of nothing else the entire time. And this scenario, sadly, has not been a one-time occurrence! Through the years, we have had multiple vacations ruined in similar manner.

The devil is good at his job, and he is also a good student of Scripture. He does not obey it, but he does observe it. He went so far as to quote it to Christ! Here is a passage that he surely knows very well:

KJV Mark 6:31 *And he said unto them, Come ye yourselves apart into a desert place, and rest a while: for there were many coming and going, and they had no leisure so much as to eat.*

Jesus taught His disciples the importance of taking time to come apart and rest. A wise old preacher once said, "If you don't come apart, you will eventually come apart!" The devil knows all of this. If he can use stress to run a man of God out of the ministry, he will. In fact, stress and discouragement are statistically the main reasons behind men leaving the ministry. The devil will try his best to stir up whatever trouble he can while the pastor is on vacation, knowing that if he succeeds, he will accomplish several things.

One: The vacation that the pastor is currently on will be ruined. In fact, that pastor will feel that he would actually have been better off not to have gone at all.

Two: The pastor will be very hesitant to take vacations in the future. I have actually skipped vacations out of fear of having a repeat of what happened while I was gone on a previous vacation.

Three: Even if the pastor does finally go on vacation again, he will be on pins and needles the entire time, wondering what is going wrong back home.

Do you see all of the damage the devil can do through one or two people that observe "Stupid People Day" while he is on vacation? Before I leave on vacation, I teasingly tell my congregation, "Please schedule any deaths or disasters for some other week." But again, deaths, injuries, unexpected surgeries, these things are not the problem or the issue. A pastor (at least a good one) will gladly interrupt or even forego entirely any vacation for something like that among his dear sheep. But when the sheep simply act in foolish or wrong ways when he is trying to rest and recuperate, they really hurt their pastor!

With that understanding, then, please allow me to give all caring church members across our land some helpful guidelines for what to do and not to do when their pastor is away.

One: Never drop a problem in the pastor's lap right before he leaves on vacation. If you do, he will think of nothing else the entire time he is gone and his vacation will be a total waste of time.

Two: Be absolutely sure that you are in church when he is gone. If you are not, he will hear about it, he will worry that something is wrong, or he will be unhappy that you are carnal, skipping church simply because he is away.

Three: No matter what happens, or how mad it makes you, do not say or do one thing about it while your pastor is away. The devil will try his best to stir up trouble specifically during that time, you need to make sure he cannot do it!

Four: Whoever is preaching while the pastor is away, even if he bores you or is not your cup of tea, make sure that not only are you there but that you openly support him and cheer him on. The pastor does not vacation well if he hears that a service was dead while he was gone.

Five: If you for some reason get upset with your pastor, do not give him any clue or hint of it before he goes, while he is gone, or for the first few days after he gets back. After he has rested, recharged, and returned, wait a few days, then come to him humbly and allow him to have a chance to explain or clarify things.

These guidelines will really help your pastor to have what he needs: a restful vacation. But before we leave the subject, please allow me to give one more helpful suggestion, this time both to the pastor and the church. It concerns what days that the pastor should be gone on vacation and why. For the average church member who works at, say, the Acme Pooch Pampering Factory, a Monday through Saturday vacation is perfectly appropriate. But if a pastor takes those exact same days, then he has not had a vacation at all! He has had six days in a hotel room somewhere to work just as hard as he would have had he never left the office.

You see, the main workday for the pastor is, of course, Sunday. On that day he will likely teach a Sunday school class, he will preach a morning message, and he will preach an evening message. Contrary to popular belief, messages do not simply pop into a preacher's head, fully formed and ready to deliver, three minutes before he goes into the pulpit. The bulk of a pastor's work week will be spent in studying and preparing for those three things on Sunday. A really well-prepared message may take anywhere from five to ten hours to prepare, sometimes more! So when a church member expects his pastor to vacation only from Monday through Saturday so he does not miss a Sunday, what that member really expects is for his pastor to not really take a vacation at all!

Every pastor may handle this a bit differently, but I like to vacation from Monday to Monday. That gives me a full week to rest, with no study necessary. I can simply read my Bible for joy during the vacation, not to try and develop a message. So, church member, please allow your pastor to have a full, uninterrupted, restful vacation, where he misses a Sunday. That can be accomplished if you and every other rational, intelligent person in the church will refuse to pick that particular time to celebrate Stupid People Day!

Chapter Eight

Special Occasions Should Be Special!

A pastor is a unique creature. He could go elsewhere and make far more money than he does in the ministry, but he doesn't. He could work a secular job, and have most of the hours of his week free, but he does not. He preaches funerals for people he does not even know, since the dearly departed is the friend of a cousin of a church member. He gets beat on by people fairly regularly and then visits those same people when they end up in the hospital, bringing flowers to them with a smile. This is a special individual we are talking about! And for a special individual, special occasions should be...special! And in this, sadly, many churches fail to do what they should. Church member, God gave you a gift when he gave you your pastor:

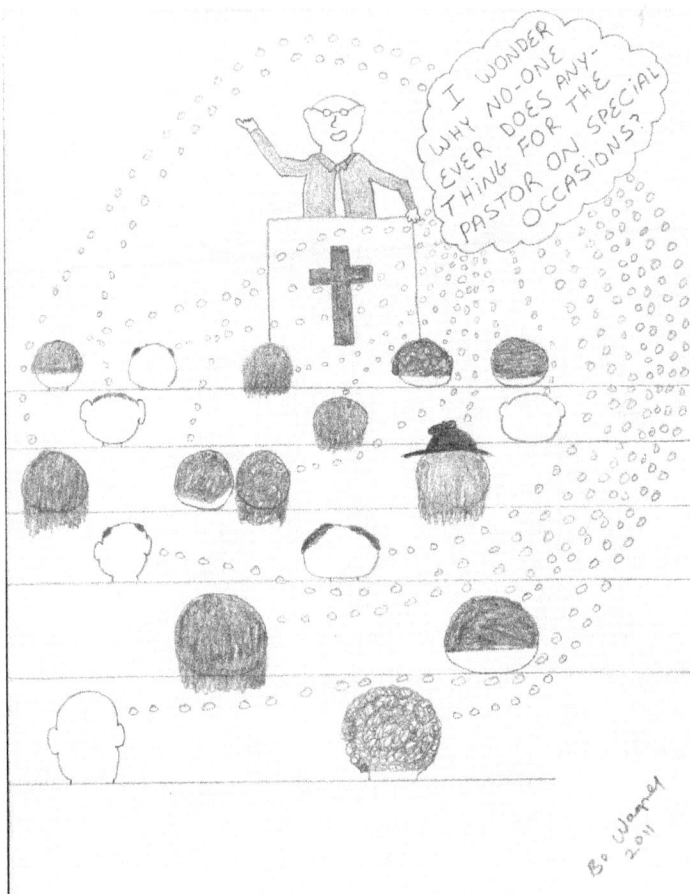

KJV Ephesians 4:8 *Wherefore he saith, When he ascended up on high, he led captivity captive, and* **gave gifts** *unto men.* **9** *(Now that he ascended, what is it but that he also descended first into the lower parts of the earth?* **10** *He that descended is the same also that ascended up far above all heavens, that he might fill all things.)* **11** *And he gave some, apostles; and some, prophets; and some, evangelists; and some, pastors and teachers;* **12** *For the perfecting of the saints, for the work of the ministry, for the edifying of the body of Christ:*

God said that He gave gifts unto men, and one of the gifts He listed was that of the pastor. So, since you have a very special person fulfilling a very special task for you, please make sure that special occasions are actually special! Make sure he and his family are treated like royalty on birthdays, anniversaries, and Christmas. Always do special things during October, which is clergy appreciation month. Every year on the anniversary of him becoming your pastor, do something special for him. The church of my teenage years gives their pastor a hundred dollars for every year he has been there. That is very good motivation for a pastor to stick around!

A pastor has the hardest job on Earth. You can make it easier by making sure that special occasions are actually special for him!

Chapter Nine

The Master of Disaster

KJV John 12:1 *Then Jesus six days before the passover came to Bethany, where Lazarus was which had been dead, whom he raised from the dead.* **2** *There they made him a supper; and Martha served: but Lazarus was one of them that sat at the table with him.* **3** *Then took Mary a pound of ointment of spikenard, very costly, and anointed the feet of Jesus, and wiped his feet with her hair: and the house was filled with the odour of the ointment.* **4** *Then saith one of his disciples, Judas Iscariot, Simon's son, which should betray him,* **5** *Why was not this ointment sold for three hundred pence, and given to the poor?* **6** *This he said, not that he cared for the poor; but because he was a thief, and had the bag, and bare what was put therein.* **7** *Then said Jesus, Let her alone: against the day of my burying hath she kept this.* **8** *For the poor always ye have with you; but me ye have not always.*

In John 12, a woman lavished upon Christ an extravagant gift. It was described as "very costly" and was estimated by Judas as being worth three hundred pence, or in our money, about a year's worth of wages for a regular laborer. The average income in America right now is regarded by many economists as being around $36,000 a year! So basically, to put it in our terms, this dear woman lavished upon Christ a gift worth roughly $36,000. And when she did, the "holy people" spoke up. Those who were "far more spiritual than Jesus" complained that the gift would have been better served being given to the poor. And who could argue with such a noble view? Jesus, that's who.

In answer to what Judas and company were saying, Jesus poked through their piety and said, "Let this woman alone!" He then pointed out that there would always, always, always be poor people, but that they would not always have the luxury of having Jesus there with them. In Mark 14:7, another account of the same event, He put it this way:

KJV Mark 14:7 *For ye have the poor with you always, and whensoever ye will ye may do them good: but me ye have not always.*

Jesus told them that they could always, any day of the week, any year of the decade, any decade of the century do good to the poor, but they had a limited time to do good to Him. Now what does this have to do with a church and their responsibility to the pastor? Plenty, friend, plenty.

NEXT SUNDAY,
THE MAIN EVENT!!!

THREE ROUNDS, CAGE MATCH, WINNER TAKES
ALL! IT'S

THE HUMBLE PASTOR

GOING UP AGAINST THE UNDEFEATED, THE
UNSTOPPABLE, THE COMPLETELY
UNREASONABLE,

THE MASTER OF
DISASTER!!!

COME SEE HIM SINK THE PASTOR'S CRUISE BY SHOWING
PICTURES OF ORPHANS, AND CRUSH THE PASTOR'S
CADILLAC BY TALKING ABOUT WAR IN THE MIDDLE
EAST!!!

Some few years back a good pastor was celebrating his 25 year anniversary as a pastor of a particular church. The church voted to send him and his wife on a cruise as a way of saying thank you for that quarter century of faithful service. But when they did, a "Master of Disaster" reared his ugly head. A master of disaster (MOD) is a person who, any time the church wants to do something extravagant for their pastor, is masterful at finding some disaster to point to as a good reason not to. This MOD stood up in church the next week, taking the pastor by complete surprise and said, "We shouldn't be wasting all this money on a cruise for the pastor when Haiti has just been leveled by an earthquake. Think of how much that money could benefit all of those poor, starving, homeless people!" The pastor, stunned, told the man he needed to sit down. He said, "I won't sit down; I'm leaving," and when we walked out, seven families that he had been secretly working on all week long walked out with him. That man, that MOD, used a disaster as a way to destroy a good man of God during the very time that his church was trying to do something nice for him.

When Jesus said, "The poor you have with you always," He was letting us know that there will never, ever be a time when there is not some type of a disaster on Earth. Either by natural or man-made disasters, every day is bad for someone somewhere! That fact does not remove from the church the duty, the right, and the privilege to lavish good upon their pastor. Especially in this age of internet and 24 hour cable news, please, tell me the last day you remember when there was not a war, or a hurricane, or a tornado, or a salmonella outbreak, or a tsunami, or an earthquake, or a famine, or, or, or, or…

What is usually very telling is that the people who are so adamant that "now is not a good time to do this for the pastor because of…" have up until that point done absolutely nothing for whatever victims they are presently crying over! Had the church not decided to give a cruise or a Cadillac or a vacation to the pastor, the MOD would never had bothered to mention the poor starving children in Somalia. He mentions them because he is jealous and wants to take something from the pastor that he himself is not receiving.

A church should take great care to recognize any MOD in their midst. And they should never allow that person to keep them from lavishing ointment upon their pastor or his family, nor should they ever allow him to make the pastor feel guilty for having that ointment lavished upon him. The poor you will have you always, but your pastor will one day be dead and gone!

I know me being in the ministry has made life hard on you guys. But no matter how many times you e-mail me the application, I am not going to try and become the next green horn on "The Deadliest Catch."

Chapter Ten

The Other People in the Glass House

Imagine this scenario: a man is created in a very unusual way. For starters, he is four-sided. Additionally, the four sides are not equal. Side one is strong, powerful, and tough. Side two is much smaller, not as powerful, much more tender. Sides three and four are smaller and weaker still. To end the description, you should know that if any of the four sides is destroyed, the entire four-sided man dies. Now suppose that this four-sided man has an enemy. This enemy wants desperately to destroy him. Where do you suppose the enemy will attack the four-sided man? The answer is obvious. He will attack one of the three weaker sides, knowing that the result will be the same as if he had actually attacked the strongest side and won.

The picture I have described actually exists in one form or another in your church. The four-sided man is the pastor! You see, the pastor does not come separate from his family. They are one multi-person unit. If the devil can destroy or discourage or somehow defeat the pastor's wife or his children, he can destroy the very ministry of the pastor himself.

But even if the pastor does not actually lose his wife or his children, just having them become so discouraged that he himself must leave the ministry for their benefit still accomplishes the devil's purpose. And the number of times that has happened is well-nigh unfathomable!

You see, the pastor knows going into things that he will live in a glass house. He is fully prepared to be watched, scrutinized, and criticized. But very often the wife and children are not prepared for those things, yet those things will happen to them as often or perhaps more often than they will happen to him. The devil knows where the weak links are, and he will attack them. A wife or children will be far easier to break under the pressure than the man of God himself.

Consider just for a few moments the unique difficulties that the pastor's wife and children face. Let us begin with the wife.

One: The pastor's wife has no one to talk to if she and her husband are struggling. She will never divulge that information to anyone in the church, and she will also never tell it to any other preacher's wife, fearing the damage done to her husband's reputation.

Two: The pastor's wife has to share her husband in ways that no other woman would ever be willing to share hers. For instance, a pastor and his family will plan a much-needed vacation, they will dream about it for months, and they will look forward to it. Then, one day into the vacation, the phone will ring (funeral home, hospital, marriage in trouble...) and the pastor will suddenly be getting into the car and driving back to the church, either taking his family with him or leaving them there by themselves. A normal wife of a worker in the pew never goes through that! Wherever he works, there is someone to cover for him when he and his family are away. Not so the pastor. No good pastor is going to tell a bereaved family member that he will "have someone fill in for him" at the funeral!

Or maybe it is the inevitable, "Yes, the moment is right!" occurrence, only to have the phone ring yet again, making the moment "wrong." This is regular in the ministry, not so much so to non-clergy.

And what of the many nights where the pastor and his dear wife are simply curled up in bed, sleeping in each other's arms, only to have a call from the hospital wake them up and demand that she spend the rest of the sleepless night alone? This is something that a pastor's wife will go through too many times to count.

Three: The pastor's wife cannot have very close friends in the church without getting accused of favoritism. Every other lady in church can but not her.

Now let us turn our attention to the unique difficulties the pastor's children will face.

One: The pastor's children face scrutiny that no other child in church faces. People often say, "Why should we treat the pastor's kids as anything special, they're just like all the other kids in church!" If that were actually true, there would be no need to treat them special. But we have already observed in a previous chapter that the kids of the pastor become viewed as "community property." Everyone else's kids are "dealt with" by their parents alone. But the pastor's kids get watched, scolded, and singled out for criticism by everybody in the church. It is not right, but it happens.

Two: The pastor's children will face the same temptations that other growing children face yet are given no room for error that other children are given. As kids move into the teen years, they begin to face the temptations and pressures that their growth provides. Sexual pressures, pressures to wear the latest styles, pressures to partake of wrong music, all of these and more face the pastor's kids. Yet, they alone, out of all the other kids in church, will be given no slack at all in any of these areas by anyone in the church.

Three: A member's child can go "bad," and it will not cause the member to lose a position as a Sunday school teacher, choir leader, what have you. But based on the qualifications of I Timothy 3, a pastor's child, at least one still at home, can cause the pastor to be unqualified to continue in the ministry, depending upon the severity of the transgression and the willingness or unwillingness of that child to repent.

So we see that "the other people in the glass house" are going to be tempting targets for the devil, because through them, he can bring down the pastor. And this brings us to the church's treatment of the pastor's family. A wise and loving church will go overboard to love and care for the pastor's wife and children. They will make a fuss over them on special occasions, they will do little things for them at random times just because they love them, and they will pray for them daily.

A church that takes care of its pastor is doing a wonderful thing. But if they neglect to care for their pastor's family, they are failing to guard the areas most likely to be targeted by the devil! In considering this truth, may I recount the observation of a good pastor friend of mine, Bryan Treadway. He has made a point through the years of talking to the godly grown up children of pastors, children who made it through the difficult childhood years in the ministry. Almost to a man or woman, they have the same story to tell. Their father's church loved them, fussed over them, and did special things for them. They made those kids glad that their father was a pastor!

As of this writing, my children are 11, 10, and 8. Even at those young ages, there have been many nights that I have held them while they cried themselves to sleep in my arms. Ministry is hard on the children of the pastor.

Church, treat your "first lady of the church" well! Make her birthdays special, remember her at Christmas and anniversaries, do sweet things for her at random times for no particular reason. Treat the kids of the pastor well; make them glad they are preacher's kids. For the sake of your pastor, take care of the other people in the glass house!

Chapter Eleven

Your Pastor Wants You to Have a Long Memory

If a pastor could bare his heart to people, here is what most of them would eventually say. One of the most hurtful things a pastor experiences in the ministry is going way above and way beyond the call of duty for people over and over and over again, only to have those same people somehow forget all about that and later blow up or bail out on him.

Throughout years in the ministry pastors will spend weeks away from home several states away in the hospital with people, only to have this happen. They will labor for free beside self-employed members when they are for some reason unable to do it all themselves, only to have this happen. They will give people money from their own pocket and from church benevolence when they are in need, only to have this happen. They will miss holidays to be in the hospital with those who are hurting, only to have this happen. They will counsel with homes that have broken up and help put them all back together, only to have this happen. They will go to court with people to help them get out of deep trouble, only to have this happen. I could list dozens and dozens more, and so could most every pastor in America! There is nothing more hurtful than to realize just how easily people forget what you have done for them through the years.

Look at a beautiful passage of Scripture with me:

KJV Hebrews 6:10 *For God is not unrighteous to forget your work and labour of love, which ye have shewed toward his name, in that ye have ministered to the saints, and do minister.*

This is amazing. The text tells us that it would actually be unrighteous of God to forget our work and labor of love in the way we have ministered to the saints. This tells me that a lot of church members across our land are unrighteous!

A pastor does not want very much from his people, but this is one thing that he does want: he wants his people to have a very long memory for what he has done for them! And when he finds such people, he cherishes them immensely. Once upon a time at our church, we had a few families get mad and leave. When they did, our dear old church Grandma, Mrs. Christine, thrilled my heart. She said, "Do they not remember when..." and she proceeded to name dates, events, dollar amounts, and other ways that we had stretched out to help those people. She remembered way, way more than I did! God bless people like that!

And now, top of the Christian Billboard Charts for the
247th straight month, "What Have You Done for Me
Lately," by the McPerry's!

We have actually given people benevolence checks, had them get angry just a day or so later and actually cash those checks *after they had blown up and left!*

Church member, a pastor deserves to build up brownie points in your mind and heart for all of the things he has done through the years. If a pastor has spent years doing good to you and your family, you are really wrong to blow up at him and leave the first time he does or says something you don't like! Be a blessing to the man of God that has been such a blessing to you; develop a very long memory for all of the things he has done for you!

Chapter Twelve

Let Me Give You an "Assist" On This One

There is a job in the church that can either be a blessing or a curse to the pastor. If it is a blessing, it is a HUGE blessing, if it is a curse, it is, well, you can figure out the rest...

The position I am speaking of is that of the Second Man, otherwise known as the Assistant Pastor, or sometimes (for very precise types) the "Assistant *to the* Pastor." This role has seen many good men, men who help the church by helping the pastor, and many bad men, men who have actually taken most of the church from their pastor and started their own, or stayed there and undermined the pastor at every turn until he quits in frustration. Pastors seem to have little trouble speaking to their church about the proper role of deacons, but for some reason most of them hesitate when it comes to informing them of the dos and don'ts of the position of the second man. So, let's take a chapter to set things straight on this issue.

To begin with, the words "Assistant Pastor" do not occur in Scripture. But for those who would use that fact to opine that it is, therefore, an unbiblical thing let me point out that the words "Sunday school" do not appear in Scripture either! Nor, in fact, do the words "Wednesday night prayer meeting" or "Sunday School Superintendent" or "Trustee" or "Committee." The fact that a word does not appear does not make something wrong.

We do find in Scripture men who fulfilled roles from which we can learn a great deal about the man that we call the second man. Good men with names like Aaron, Hur, Elisha, and John the Baptist. But also bad men with names like Korah, Gehazi, Absalom, and Judas.

To begin with, let us look at Aaron. He is a unique case in that he truly was both a good assistant and also a bad assistant! Studying his life in the Scripture, we find that for the most part he was loyal, honest, helpful, and true. But then we find that in Exodus 32, he made a terrible mistake:

KJV Exodus 32:1 And when the people saw that Moses delayed to come down out of the mount, the people gathered themselves together unto Aaron, and said unto him, Up, make us gods, which shall go before us; for as for this Moses, the man that brought us up out of the land of Egypt, we wot not what is become of him. 2 And Aaron said unto them, Break off the golden earrings, which are in the ears of your wives, of your sons, and of your daughters, and bring them unto me. 3 And all the people brake off the golden earrings which were in their ears, and brought them unto Aaron. 4 And he received them at their hand, and fashioned it with a graving tool, after he had made it a molten calf: and they said, These be thy gods, O Israel, which brought thee up out of the land of Egypt. 5 And when Aaron saw it, he built an altar before it; and Aaron made proclamation, and said, To morrow is a feast to the LORD.

While Moses the man of God was away, Aaron, the "second man," gave in to pressure from the congregation and did something that Moses would never have allowed. A church needs to understand that the second man is under the authority of the pastor. He is a hired employee just like a janitor or a custodian. He is to do things the way of the man of God, not his own way, and not the way of the congregation. And lest someone say, "Wait a minute, shouldn't he do things the way he believes God would have him to do them?" let me show you this:

KJV Exodus 4:14 *And the anger of the LORD was kindled against Moses, and he said, Is not Aaron the Levite thy brother? I know that he can speak well. And also, behold, he cometh forth to meet thee: and when he seeth thee, he will be glad in his heart. 15 **And thou shalt speak unto him, and put words in his mouth**: and I will be with thy mouth, and with his mouth, and will teach you what ye shall do. 16 And he shall be thy spokesman unto the people: and he shall be, even he shall be to thee instead of a mouth, and **thou shalt be to him instead of God**.*

If you had accused Moses of "putting words in Aaron's mouth," he would have said, "Of course I do!" If you had accused Moses of "acting like God" to Aaron he would have said, "Of course I do!" It is in black and white, in God's own handwriting!

I understand that this, as well as anything else, can be abused. But that does not change the fact that the pastor hears from God and then the assistant hears from the pastor. It was not Moses and Aaron hearing from God; it was Moses hearing from God, and Aaron hearing from Moses. It was not Moses and Aaron both saying what was on their hearts; it was both Aaron and Moses saying what was on Moses' heart.

The second man is in a unique position in the church. Any regular member can say or think what they want, but the assistant is to say and think the words and thoughts of the man of God. No wonder so few men can ever truly fulfill this role; it is actually in some ways much harder than the role of the pastor. It certainly takes more humility than the role of the pastor!

But that episode with the golden calf was Aaron on his worst day. There was another day when he and a man named Hur (try saying that three times fast: he and a man named Hur...) both acted as very good assistants:

KJV Exodus 17:10 *So Joshua did as Moses had said to him, and fought with Amalek: and Moses, Aaron, and Hur went up to the top of the hill.* **11** *And it came to pass, when Moses held up his hand, that Israel prevailed: and when he let down his hand, Amalek prevailed.* **12** *But Moses' hands were heavy; and they took a stone, and put it under him, and he sat thereon;*

and Aaron and Hur stayed up his hands, the one on the one side, and the other on the other side; and his hands were steady until the going down of the sun.

This is a good description of the role of the assistant. Hold up the hands of the man of God! These men were not "other Moseses," they were people to hold up the hands of Moses. An assistant pastor is not another pastor; he is a person to hold up the hands of the pastor. When a church begins to look to an assistant instead of the pastor, both the assistant and the church are showing that they do not understand the proper role of the second man.

Let us look at another good example of an assistant, a man who later became famous in his own right, a man named Elisha.

KJV 1 Kings 19:19 *So he departed thence, and found Elisha the son of Shaphat, who was plowing with twelve yoke of oxen before him, and he with the twelfth: and Elijah passed by him, and cast his mantle upon him.* **20** *And he left the oxen, and ran after Elijah, and said, Let me, I pray thee, kiss my father and my mother, and then I will follow thee. And he said unto him, Go back again: for what have I done to thee?* **21** *And he returned back from him, and took a yoke of oxen, and slew them, and boiled their flesh with the instruments of the oxen, and gave unto the people, and they did eat. Then he arose, and went after Elijah, and ministered unto him.*

*Assistant Pastor Jones has informed me that he will
not be here today, as he has something important
to dig into.*

It is clear from this passage that Elisha's job was not to serve the people; it was to serve the prophet. Elisha ministered to Elijah! And he did so in ways that were not at all glorious.

KJV 2 Kings 3:11 *But Jehoshaphat said, Is there not here a prophet of the LORD, that we may enquire of the LORD by him? And one of the king of Israel's servants answered and said, Here is Elisha the son of Shaphat, which poured water on the hands of Elijah.*

Elisha's job was to pour water on the hands of Elijah. Can you imagine most modern assistants being willing to fulfill this role?

Hey, Assistant Arnold, I am going to wash my hands. Come and turn the faucet on for me, and then turn it off again when I am finished!

I am guessing that Assistant Arnold would protest that such a task was demeaning. And in so doing, he would be showing that he does not have the right spirit to be an assistant. An assistant should be one that does whatever physical, menial tasks are necessary to lighten the load of the man of God. And once again, please understand that, as clearly seen by I Kings 19:21, it is not the job of the second man to serve the people; it is the job of the second man to serve the pastor. He is not another pastor for the people; he is a servant for the one and only pastor the people have.

Another good example to look to in considering the role of the second man is John the Baptist.

KJV Mark 1:1 *The beginning of the gospel of Jesus Christ, the Son of God; 2 As it is written in the prophets, Behold, I send my messenger before thy face, which shall prepare thy way before thee. 3 The voice of one crying in the wilderness, Prepare ye the way of the Lord, make his paths straight. 4 John did baptize in the wilderness, and preach the baptism of repentance for the remission of sins. 5 And there went out unto him all the land of Judaea, and they of Jerusalem, and were all baptized of him in the river of Jordan, confessing their sins. 6 And John was clothed with camel's hair, and with a girdle of a skin about his loins; and he did eat locusts and wild honey; 7 And preached, saying, There cometh one mightier than I after me, the latchet of whose shoes I am not worthy to stoop down and unloose.*

KJV John 3:27 *John answered and said, A man can receive nothing, except it be given him from heaven. 28 Ye yourselves bear me witness, that I said, I am not the Christ, but that I am sent before him. 29 He that hath the bride is the bridegroom: but the friend of the bridegroom, which standeth and heareth him, rejoiceth greatly because of the bridegroom's voice: this my joy therefore is fulfilled. 30 He must increase, but I must decrease.*

In both of these passages, John was the second man to the greatest pastor that ever lived, Jesus Himself. And John proved himself as one of the greatest assistants that ever lived when he continually elevated the One he worked for. The role of the assistant should ever be to elevate the pastor, to make much of the pastor in the eyes of the people. He should be the pastor's biggest fan and most vocal cheerleader.

But after considering these good second men, we would be remiss not to examine some of the bad second men of Scripture. Let us begin with a man named Korah:

KJV Numbers 16:1 *Now Korah, the son of Izhar, the son of Kohath, the son of Levi, and Dathan and Abiram, the sons of Eliab, and On, the son of Peleth, sons of Reuben, took men:* **2** *And they rose up before Moses, with certain of the children of Israel, two hundred and fifty princes of the assembly, famous in the congregation, men of renown:* **3** *And they gathered themselves together against Moses and against Aaron, and said unto them, Ye take too much upon you, seeing all the congregation are holy, every one of them, and the LORD is among them: wherefore then lift ye up yourselves above the congregation of the LORD?*

This was perhaps the first ever rebellion by a second man. Korah sounded good, and he was careful to couch his rebellion in religious terms, but there was nothing right about him. He led a rebellion against the man that God had placed in charge, and that rebellion cost him his life. He accused Moses falsely, and God had the earth swallow him alive into Hell. God will be patient with many things, but He will not usually be patient with an assistant rising up against the pastor!

And then we find a man named Gehazi:

KJV 2 Kings 5:16 *But he said, As the LORD liveth, before whom I stand, I will receive none. And he urged him to take it; but he refused.* **17** *And Naaman said, Shall there not then, I pray thee, be given to thy servant two mules' burden of earth? for thy servant will henceforth offer neither burnt offering nor sacrifice unto other gods, but unto the LORD.* **18** *In this thing the LORD pardon thy servant, that when my master goeth into the house of Rimmon to worship there, and he leaneth on my hand, and I bow myself in the house of Rimmon: when I bow down myself in the house of Rimmon, the LORD pardon thy servant in this thing.* **19** *And he said unto him, Go in peace. So he departed from him a little way.* **20** *But Gehazi, the servant of Elisha the man of God, said, Behold, my master hath spared Naaman this Syrian, in not receiving at his hands that which he brought: but, as the LORD liveth, I will run after him, and take somewhat of him.* **21** *So Gehazi followed after Naaman. And when Naaman saw him running after him, he lighted down from the chariot to meet him, and said, Is all well?* **22** *And he said, All is well. My master hath sent me, saying, Behold, even now there be come to me from mount Ephraim two young men of the sons of the prophets: give them, I pray thee, a talent of silver, and two changes of garments.* **23** *And Naaman said, Be content, take two talents. And he urged him, and bound two talents of silver in two bags, with two changes of garments, and laid them upon two of his servants; and they bare them before him.* **24** *And when he came to the tower, he took them from their hand, and bestowed them in the house: and he let the* *men go, and they departed. **25** But he went in, and stood before his master. And Elisha said unto him, Whence comest thou, Gehazi? And he said, Thy servant went no whither. **26** And he said unto him, Went not mine heart with thee, when the man turned again from his chariot to meet thee? Is it a time to receive money, and to receive garments, and oliveyards, and vineyards, and sheep, and oxen, and menservants, and maidservants? **27** The leprosy therefore of Naaman shall cleave unto thee, and unto thy seed for ever. And he went out from his presence a leper as white as snow.*

The occasion of this chapter was the healing of Naaman. After he was healed, he offered money and rewards to Elisha, who had graduated from being the assistant to actually being the man of God after Elijah was taken. Elisha refused that money. But the second man, Gehazi, ran after Naaman and took some anyway.

What happened was a good ancient example of a problem that still exists in modern times between pastors and assistants. The pastor has one way of doing something in his mind, and the assistant has another way of doing that something in his mind, and rather than deferring to the pastor, he does it his own way, following the judgment of his own heart. Second men need to understand that it is never right to do things their way. God did not put them in charge of anything. God put the pastor in charge; the assistant is to do things the pastor's way, and if the pastor does wrong, God will be the One to deal with him. Short of heresy or immorality or gross wickedness of some kind, the assistant must understand that he follows the pastor, period.

Now let us turn our attention to Assistant Pastor Absalom:

KJV 2 Samuel 15:1 *And it came to pass after this, that Absalom prepared him chariots and horses, and fifty men to run before him.* **2** *And Absalom rose up early, and stood beside the way of the gate: and it was so, that when any man that had a controversy came to the king for judgment, then Absalom called unto him, and said, Of what city art thou? And he said, Thy servant is of one of the tribes of Israel.* **3** *And Absalom said unto him, See, thy matters are good and right; but there is no man deputed of the king to hear thee.* **4** *Absalom said moreover, Oh that I were made judge in the land, that every man which hath any suit or cause might come unto me, and I would do him justice!* **5** *And it was so, that when any man came nigh to him to do him obeisance, he put forth his hand, and took him, and kissed him.* **6** *And on this manner did Absalom to all Israel that came to the king for judgment: so Absalom stole the hearts of the men of Israel.*

In the case of Absalom, we have an "Assistant" that intentionally stole the kingdom from the one who was rightfully in charge. He did so by intercepting people coming to David and subtly planting doubts in their mind about David. He then told those people whatever they wanted to hear and how much better off they would be if he was in charge. This scenario has been played out a thousand times over in churches all across the land.

Some years back, I preached a revival for a dear old man of God who heard me preach at a jubilee meeting. I could tell he had a sadness about him, but I did not know why. Very soon I found out. When I went to preach the revival for him, I found a large, beautiful church. He had started the work from scratch and spent decades building it. But I soon saw that there were a relatively small number of members. A few months earlier, his assistant of many years had taken most of his members and started a new church with them! The old pastor had not been involved in any type of wrongdoing, he had not preached heresy, he had just gotten old, and a younger, stronger man, his assistant, took his church.

An Absalom such as this may not die under God's judgment quite as quickly or dramatically as Absalom did...but then again he might! Such wickedness is unfathomable. Church member, wherever you are, listen to me: if the second man at your church demonstrates even the *tiniest* amount of disloyalty to your pastor, you need to go warn your pastor immediately, and you need to inform the second man that you will be watching him like a hawk!

And now we come to the most infamous second man of all, a man who was so respectable as to be viewed in a positive light by absolutely everyone. His name was Judas Iscariot.

KJV John 13:21 *When Jesus had thus said, he was troubled in spirit, and testified, and said, Verily, verily, I say unto you, that one of you shall betray me.* **22** *Then the disciples looked one on another, doubting*

of whom he spake. **23** *Now there was leaning on Jesus'*
bosom one of his disciples, whom Jesus loved. **24** *Simon*
Peter therefore beckoned to him, that he should ask
who it should be of whom he spake. **25** *He then lying on*
Jesus' breast saith unto him, Lord, who is it? **26** *Jesus*
answered, He it is, to whom I shall give a sop, when I
have dipped it. And when he had dipped the sop, he
gave it to Judas Iscariot, the son of Simon. **27** *And after*
the sop Satan entered into him. Then said Jesus unto
him, That thou doest, do quickly. **28** *Now no man at the*
table knew for what intent he spake this unto him. **29**
For some of them thought, because Judas had the bag,
that Jesus had said unto him, Buy those things that we
have need of against the feast; or, that he should give
something to the poor. **30** *He then having received the*
sop went immediately out: and it was night.

It always amazes me to realize just how openly
Jesus pointed to Judas as His betrayer, only to see that
not one of the disciples believed it! He said *whoever I*
give the sop to, it is him, and then He gave the sop to
Judas! How can that be missed?

Judas, you see, was the best deceiver that ever
lived in human form. Everyone regarded him as kind,
meek, gentle, humble, honest, loyal–pick a good
adjective and he would be regarded as that! In fact, in
all of his history with Jesus and the other disciples, he
only gave one tiny clue as to any disloyalty in his heart,
and that was about money:

KJV John 12:1 *Then Jesus six days before the*
passover came to Bethany, where Lazarus was which
had been dead, whom he raised from the dead. **2** *There*

they made him a supper; and Martha served: but Lazarus was one of them that sat at the table with him. 3 Then took Mary a pound of ointment of spikenard, very costly, and anointed the feet of Jesus, and wiped his feet with her hair: and the house was filled with the odour of the ointment. 4 Then saith one of his disciples, Judas Iscariot, Simon's son, which should betray him, 5 Why was not this ointment sold for three hundred pence, and given to the poor? 6 This he said, not that he cared for the poor; but because he was a thief, and had the bag, and bare what was put therein.

This money complaint was the only clue that Judas ever gave. As such, the other disciples regarded him as the best of the best, but Jesus clearly knew better.

My father-in-law and I preached a revival together some years ago. The pastor and his assistant took us out to dinner after church one night. At that dinner, there came a moment when the pastor went to the buffet bar, and we were left sitting with the assistant. The assistant began to confide in us that some men in the church were complaining to him about the pastor. I asked him how the pastor was taking it, and he said, "Oh, he doesn't know, I haven't told him."

I was stunned. I said, "Sir, you need to tell your pastor all of this immediately!"

He said, "Oh I can't do that, these people spoke to me in confidence; I won't even tell you who they are." This man had allowed himself to be placed in a position where he was being loyal to members rather than to his pastor.

The next day, we pulled the pastor aside and informed him that he not only had unseen problems with some folks in the church but that his own assistant was disloyal. His jaw dropped, and he didn't want to believe us. After all, we were just visiting preachers. This other man was his very own assistant! Alas, it was not many more months until the man lost his church, undone by a rebellion led by his members, with a disloyal assistant pastor as their main tool.

From all of the examples in Scripture and practical experience, positive and negative, it is evident that the role of the second man can either be a huge blessing or a huge curse to the church. But since this book is written to church members, trying to say what the pastor wishes he could say, please let me give you a conclusion to this chapter that does just that.

Please remember that there is only one pastor in the church. The assistant is not "another pastor" or "a little pastor," he is simply a servant to the one and only pastor that the church has. His job is to make the pastor's life easier, to serve the pastor, to back the pastor, to be loyal to the pastor. He is never to come between you and the pastor. He is never to listen to your complaints about how the pastor is doing things. He is never to undermine the pastor in any way. If a second man will not be what he should and insists on being what he should not, then your pastor should remove him, and you should back your pastor 100% when he does so.

Chapter Thirteen

Revive Us Again to Members Who Understand the Benefits of Their Pastor Preaching Revivals!

In chapter two, we dealt a bit with the pastor who from time to time preaches revival meetings. But this subject truly deserves a chapter unto itself, so here goes.

To begin with, allow me to reiterate the principle that I laid out in chapter two. A full time pastor should be just like a church member in that he should be allowed to have his free time, and to do with it whatever he chooses. If a member works forty hours and then chooses to earn extra money mowing lawns in his free time, so be it! If a pastor works forty hours and then chooses to earn extra money preaching a revival in his free time, so be it! If a member works forty hours and then chooses to spend his free time driving up to the mountains and getting a hotel, so be it. If a pastor works forty hours and then chooses to spend his time in

105

a hotel in a podunk town so he can preach in a little church who wants a revival meeting, so be it. If a member wants to work 80 hours one week so he can have the entire next week off to go to the beach, so be it. If a pastor wants to work 80 hours one week so that he can have the entire next week off to preach a revival in West Virginia, so be it. Have an even scale, let things be the same for the pastor as they are for the members!

But every church member should also clearly understand that the pastor, even when he is off preaching a revival meeting somewhere, will still actually put in a good 40 hours or more of work for his church. As I explained in chapter two, when I recently preached a revival in Fayetteville, NC, I still worked 42 hours for my church in Mooresboro, NC! A pastor will work all day on Sunday before he leaves for revival, he will normally work part of the day on Monday, he will carry his work with him to the hotel and prepare all week for the next Sunday, and he will probably work most of the day Saturday when he gets back. Anyone who complains about the pastor "taking a salary from the church even though he isn't working" while he preaches a revival has no earthly idea what he is talking about!

Church members who work regular jobs have benefits that any pastor would envy. If they work more than 40 hours, they get time and a half. If they don't, they get "comp time," meaning that every hour they work over 40 is an hour that is saved up and can be used later to do whatever he wants and still get paid for it. After 14 years as a pastor working 70 and 80 hour weeks, if I got comp time, I could take the next decade off and still get paid for it!

But no pastor wants that. What a pastor does want is the ability to go and preach meetings somewhere without having someone back home gripe and complain about it as if the pastor is somehow doing something wrong. He isn't! And, dear church member, if your pastor has to be physically present in your town 24 hours a day, you don't expect your pastor to be a pastor, you expect him to be a nanny!

Most people these days cannot really understand something unless it somehow benefits them. The good news is, this actually does. I can show you, quite clearly, that your pastor preaching revival meetings actually benefits your church. I am going to give you a list of benefits that I personally know of, and I encourage you to memorize and never forget them.

One: When your pastor preaches revival meetings, he and your church become better known. This leads to having people who move to your area come and join your church, since they already like to hear your pastor preach. We have several families at Cornerstone who heard me preach in other places before they ever visited my church.

Two: Other churches will put you and your pastor on their prayer list. My church and I have literally thousands of people across the world praying for us on a daily basis because they have heard me

Flat tires, car chained to the ground, gas tank welded shut, club on the steering wheel. . .Oh that's right! I told the church I was preaching a revival next week.

preach in revival meetings, and I have asked them to put us on their prayer list.

Three: Other churches will, from time to time, actually help your church with needs in response to your pastor preaching a revival meeting. I preached at a church in South Carolina during our building project, and that church gave my church $1000.00 to help with our building. I preached a revival in West Virginia and their church a year later gave our church an amazing baby grand piano that is still used every service in our church! I preached a meeting in Concord, NC, and met the Craftsmen for Christ, who later spent five months helping us in our building project.

Four: Your pastor will meet other Christian young men and ladies who are single, and the Lord will lay on his heart someone from your church to set them up with. Many, many marriages have come out of this arrangement!

Five: Your pastor will have some of his needs met, encouraging him, and when he is encouraged, you will be encouraged.

Six: Above all, your pastor will win souls to the Lord, and every soul he wins as a result of you allowing him to preach revivals without difficulty from you is a soul that will go on your account! I preached a revival in Thomasville some months back, where more than 50 people came to know Christ as their Savior. Every member of my church who prayed rather than pouted about me preaching that meeting shares in all of those souls saved!

Church member, your pastor not only has the right to preach revival meetings, he has the right to do so with your full support! And this is not opinion, it is Bible. Look at what Paul told a young pastor named Timothy:

KJV 2 Timothy 4:5 *But watch thou in all things, endure afflictions, **do the work of an evangelist**, make full proof of thy ministry.*

A pastor was told to do the work of an evangelist. Truthfully, some of the very best evangelists are pastors. They understand the local church and are far less likely to do harm than people who have never pastored. A pastor, as an evangelist, will be very unlikely to ever "blow in, blow up, and blow out" as some evangelists are prone to do. A pastor's first responsibility is to his own flock, but a church should still delight in their pastor preaching revivals, and never, ever give him any difficulty over him so doing!

Chapter Fourteen

Your Pastor Is There During Your Storms, You Be There During His

Looking at the life of Paul, it is almost impossible not to feel sorry for him from time to time. Especially when we read things like this:

KJV 2 Timothy 4:10 *For Demas hath forsaken me, having loved this present world, and is departed unto Thessalonica; Crescens to Galatia, Titus unto Dalmatia.*

KJV 2 Timothy 4:16 *At my first answer no man stood with me, but all men forsook me: I pray God that it may not be laid to their charge*

Paul was one who stood for Christ and for Christians, no matter what the cost to himself. And it certainly was a high cost for him:

KJV Acts 20:18 *And when they were come to him, he said unto them, Ye know, from the first day that I came into Asia, after what manner I have been with you at all seasons,* **19** *Serving the Lord with all humility of mind, and with many tears, and temptations, which* *befell me by the lying in wait of the Jews:* **20** *And how I kept back nothing that was profitable unto you, but have shewed you, and have taught you publickly, and from house to house,* **21** *Testifying both to the Jews, and also to the Greeks, repentance toward God, and faith toward our Lord Jesus Christ.* **22** *And now, behold, I go bound in the spirit unto Jerusalem, not knowing the things that shall befall me there:* **23** *Save that the Holy Ghost witnesseth in every city, saying that bonds and afflictions abide me.* **24** *But none of these things move me, neither count I my life dear unto myself, so that I might finish my course with joy, and the ministry, which I have received of the Lord Jesus, to testify the gospel of the grace of God.*

Paul's ministry was marked by being faithful and loyal through a tremendous amount of physical and emotional pain and suffering. But alas, it was also marked by him being forsaken by those he had helped! Every pastor knows this same heartache. Church member, your pastor has likely been there for you through the worst storms of your life. He has held you in the hospital room when the doctor said, "I'm sorry, there is nothing we can do." He has wept with you through the agony of a bitter divorce. He has spent hour upon hour with you helping to fix your marriage. He has been there when your house burned down, when you lost your job, when you wrecked your car, when you broke your bones, and when you were just inexplicably depressed.

Got you covered, Pastor!

Bo Wagner
2015

Your pastor is the one who will cut short a vacation and rush back to the hospital to be by your bedside. He is the one who will loan you his car when yours falls apart. He is the one who will lie on his face in the floor praying for your wayward child to come home.

Your pastor, though, is also human like you. As such, he will have storms in his life just like you have storms in yours! And just like he was there for you in your storms, you should determine now to be there for him in his storms. Pastor Paul had some that surely did:

KJV 2 Timothy 1:16 *The Lord give mercy unto the house of Onesiphorus; for he oft refreshed me, and was not ashamed of my chain.*

Whoever Onesiphorous was, God bless him, and may every pastor have a church full of members just like him!

Sir, ma'am, one day your pastor may encounter the storm of financial difficulties. You be there for him like he always is for you. One day your pastor may encounter the storm of having a bunch of people leave church. Don't you be one of them. You be there for him like he always is for you. One day your pastor may encounter the storm of having someone criticize him. You be there for him like he always is for you.

There are an infinite number of storms a pastor may face. The devil hates men of God, and he knows that if he can bring them down, others will fall along with him, and the work of God will be severely damaged. Stand with him so that he is able to weather the storm! We once went through a storm that really shook us to the core. Through it, we had a great many people step up and stand alongside us. They called us every day to check on us, they took us to lunch to encourage us, they sent us text messages to make us smile, they dared anyone to attack us, these people will never, ever, know what they meant to us in those awful hours!

A member who has had a pastor stand with them through their storms ought to be first in line to stand with a pastor in his.

Chapter Fifteen

Loyalty: More Precious than Rubies!

Pop Quiz! Finish these phrases: Batman and _____. The Lone Ranger and _____.

That was easy, wasn't it! Robin and Tonto never had top billing, but they will never be forgotten either. But have you ever tried to put your finger on why? Think about it. Robin was, in reality, an annoying little twerp. He wore funny clothes, he always got himself into trouble that Batman had to get him out of, and he had a whiny sort of voice. Tonto had a limited vocabulary and poor people skills. So why do we remember them? One word–Loyalty! Robin and Tonto could be counted on, period. If you messed with the boss, you messed with them.

If you were to put a suitcase with a million dollars in it on one side of the church, and on the other side of the church a bunch of people who would be guaranteed to always be loyal to the pastor, I promise you that the vast majority of pastors would ignore that suitcase full

Loyalty ...

You won't get to my pastor without getting through me first!

of cash and go diving headfirst into the crowd of loyal people!

You see, pastors understand what Solomon taught:

KJV Proverbs 25:19 *Confidence in an unfaithful man in time of trouble is like a broken tooth, and a foot out of joint.*

Expecting people to be there for you and with you and then realizing that you were wrong is a terrible sort of pain! Loyalty is utterly priceless. And it is not something that has to be developed over decades either; it can come quickly and be very beneficial. One of my favorite examples of that in the Bible is a man named Ittai.

KJV 2 Samuel 15:14 *And David said unto all his servants that were with him at Jerusalem, Arise, and let us flee; for we shall not else escape from Absalom: make speed to depart, lest he overtake us suddenly, and bring evil upon us, and smite the city with the edge of the sword.* **15** *And the king's servants said unto the king, Behold, thy servants are ready to do whatsoever my lord the king shall appoint.* **16** *And the king went forth, and all his household after him. And the king left ten women, which were concubines, to keep the house.* **17** *And the king went forth, and all the people after him, and tarried in a place that was far off.* **18** *And all his servants passed on beside him; and all the Cherethites, and all the Pelethites, and all the Gittites, six hundred men which came after him from Gath, passed on before the king.* **19** *Then said the king to Ittai the Gittite, Wherefore goest thou also with us? return to thy place,* *and abide with the king: for thou art a stranger, and also an exile.* **20** *Whereas thou camest but yesterday, should I this day make thee go up and down with us? seeing I go whither I may, return thou, and take back thy brethren: mercy and truth be with thee.* **21** *And Ittai answered the king, and said, As the LORD liveth, and as my lord the king liveth, surely in what place my lord the king shall be, whether in death or life, even there also will thy servant be.* **22** *And David said to Ittai, Go and pass over. And Ittai the Gittite passed over, and all his men, and all the little ones that were with him.*

During the rebellion of Absalom, a man came to David to help. His name was Ittai the Gittite. He had just arrived the day before, not realizing that trouble was brewing! David told him that he could go back home, that this was not his trouble. Ittai's response was beautiful:

KJV 2 Samuel 15:21 *And Ittai answered the king, and said, As the LORD liveth, and as my lord the king liveth, surely in what place my lord the king shall be, whether in death or life, even there also will thy servant be.*

That, dear church member, is loyalty! To put it in more modern terms, and in the context of the church, it would go something like this:

As the Lord liveth, Pastor, wherever you go, I'm there. If you get kicked out, I'm gone too. If 60 percent of the people leave, I'll be in the 40 percent that stay. If someone tries

120

to beat you up, they have to come through me to do it. This thing is till death do us part!

That is loyalty! I have often observed that loyalty is in very short supply anymore. If a pastor has not gone into immorality or gross wickedness, if he has not preached heresy, he ought to be able to expect loyalty. Previous generations had that, this present one not so much so. That is a shame, because loyalty truly is more precious than rubies!

Chapter Sixteen

The Golden Years

I am now going to write about something in which I have absolutely no experience. Do you hear me, you sarcastic whippersnappers? I am just now experiencing the forties, which makes me decades and decades away from the golden years. No matter that my hair is already starting to show gray, back already aching, memory already fading...

Paul the apostle was able, at one stage of his life, to say what we all hope to eventually be able to say:

KJV Philemon 1:9 *Yet for love's sake I rather beseech thee, being such an one as* **Paul the aged***, and now also a prisoner of Jesus Christ.*

Paul managed to make it in the ministry until he became an old man! He went from young and fiery to old and seasoned during the course of his ministry. I have been very blessed in my few years to get to know some wonderful, beautiful, precious old men of God:

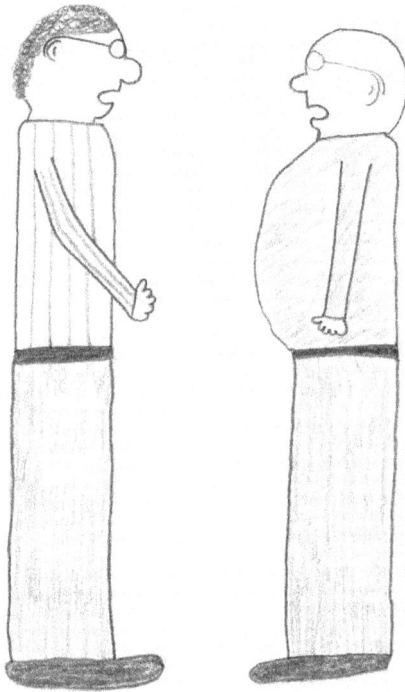

"We had to let Reverend Smith go this week."
"What for? Adultery? Embezzlement? Heresy?"
"Worse, he turned 70!"

Albert Hardin, Herbert Adams, James Ellis, Fred Baynard and others. These old men are dear to me!

I have also, through the years, been able to see that churches often react very differently to the golden years of their pastor. Some are treated like royalty, revered, respected, and rewarded for their decades of faithful service. Some, though, are shifted aside like burdens, and gotten to the curb as soon as it can be arranged. I cannot even bring myself to pray for God to have mercy on churches that do that to a good old man of God!

Throughout the Bible, the aged in general are shown to be objects of great respect:

KJV Leviticus 19:32 *Thou shalt rise up before the hoary head, and honour the face of the old man, and fear thy God: I am the LORD.*

If this is true of old men in general, how much more should it be true of an old man of God! Church member, hear me: take good care of your old pastor. Begin to take good care of your old pastor while he is still a young pastor by starting and funding a good retirement account for him. If you do that one simple thing, his golden years will not have to be spent eating beans and rice and hoping for enough social security money to keep his lights on! Many years ago at the church in which I was a teenager, the church started putting $500 a month into the pastor's retirement account. When he reaches his seventies, he will be well off, and that church has been blessed because of what they have done!

You should, furthermore, take care of your old pastor by ensuring him, preferably in writing, that should he die first, you will take steps to take care of his widow. Let the man die without worrying on his death bed what will happen to his beloved spouse whom he labored beside for five or six decades of ministry!

But do not stop there. While he is in his golden years, allow him to put enough good staff around him to keep him as the pastor as long as he is able to do it. Allow him to hire an assistant or a youth pastor or a custodian or whatever he needs to make sure that he can do the basic tasks of praying and preaching.

Let him take more vacations than ever. Send him to the places he always wanted to go but could not. Put him in a Cadillac to travel in. Make sure his grass stays cut.

Take care also to rally around him as he changes with age. When his speech slows, when his energy fades, remember that this is the same man that gave his entire youthful store of years and energy in serving you! Cheer him on, shout for him, love him, and let him run the last few miles of his race with you running beside him, cheering him on the entire way. The day will come when he is gone, and you once again have a youthful pastor. But don't rush that day. You make sure that every moment of every day of the golden years for your pastor truly are golden!

Chapter Seventeen

Beyond the Grave

May I make a confession to you that perhaps every other pastor would cop to as well if you pushed them? I often wonder what things will be like in my church after I die and will they even remember me. Will they let some new guy come in and bad mouth the way I always did things? Will the new guy take down any pictures of me? Will the members ever go back and listen to my old messages?

These things may not seem important to you, but they are to long-term pastors. No church should ever dwell in the past, and no new pastor should ever feel like he is pastoring in the shadow of the man who died before him. But every pastor ought to be assured that he will be remembered, loved, and respected even beyond the grave. You see, every pastor wants the testimony of Abel:

KJV Hebrews 11:4 *By faith Abel offered unto God a more excellent sacrifice than Cain, by which he* *obtained witness that he was righteous, God testifying of his gifts: and by it **he being dead yet speaketh**.*

Every pastor wants to know that he has had an impact large enough that he will not be forgotten or minimized after he has gone to his reward. And there is only one way to let him know that: tell him while he is still alive! When a pastor has reached the age where he could die without anyone being shocked, a loving church should, more than ever before, take time to let him know how much he means to them. They should recount for him messages that he has preached that have changed their lives. They should thank him regularly for all that he has done for them through the years. A wise man once said:

Give your flowers while they're livin', so your knowin' where their goin'.

When the man of God has then gone to his reward, know that he is part of that great cloud of witnesses that Hebrews tells us of. Know that he is still watching with interest! Never make your new pastor labor under the pressure to be just like him, but never allow any new pastor to mock or minimize him either. Take good care of your pastor, even beyond the grave!

"Pastor was pretty serious about things staying on course after his death."

www.ingramcontent.com/pod-product-compliance
Lightning Source LLC
Chambersburg PA
CBHW060940040426
42445CB00011B/950